Eating Disorders

WHEN FOOD TURNS AGAINST YOU

BY BEN SONDER

FRANKLIN WATTS

NEW YORK o CHICAGO o
LONDON o TORONTO o SYDNEY

Library of Congress Cataloging-in-Publication Data

Sonder, Ben, 1954–
    Eating disorders : when food turns against you / by Ben Sonder.
      p. cm.
    Includes bibliographical references and index.
    Summary: Examines such eating disorders as bulimia and anorexia
nervosa and discusses possible causes and available treatment.
    ISBN 0-531-11175-X
    1. Eating disorders—Juvenile literature. [1. Eating disorders.]
I. Title.
RC552.E18S59   1993
616.85'26—dc20   92-37547 CIP AC

CONTENTS

Eating Disorders

BODY VERSUS MIND

It's almost as if our bodies and our minds were two different eaters—two people who sometimes clash with each other and sometimes come to a happy agreement. Within this "odd couple," one eater is wise and always eats to live. The other eater seeks food to live as well—but also for other complicated, sometimes contradictory, reasons.

FOOD
AS FUEL

Your body has perfect judgment when it comes to the kinds and amounts of food you need. It uses exactly the right amount of food for fuel, then either stores or eliminates what's left over.

Glossy advertisements, food colorants, packaging, or artificial flavorings cannot swerve your body from its course of efficient use of food. And through the process of digestion, the body discovers all of food's hidden ingredients.

The moment an appetizingly prepared piece of food, such as a piece of chocolate layer cake with a dab of whipped cream, enters the human mouth, it ceases to be what attracted the eater and becomes instead a chemical substance. First, the taste buds bring messages about it to the brain. If these messages match certain categories the brain has learned to recognize as "good," the flow of saliva in the mouth increases. Saliva immediately begins working on starches in the food, breaking them down into simple sugars. At the same time, the teeth grind the food into a more manageable lump called a *bolus.*

In the stomach, the breakdown into simpler chemicals continues. Here, food loses the odor, texture, and taste that originally appealed to you. The bolus is churned and kneaded into a sour mash of food and stomach acids. These acids are so strong they would immediately burn through your flesh if not protected by the mucus-coated folds of your stomach lining. The acids break the food down still further. From this sour mash, proteins, carbohydrates, and other substances can more easily be removed and absorbed.

In the intestines, bacteria break down the food even further. The process continues relentlessly until little is left of the food that the body can use. At the end of this digestive line, the leftovers are ejected to keep the body from being poisoned.

The identical process takes place each time someone eats, regardless of what the eater puts into her or his body—grand cuisine or fast food. Because the body is programmed to know its needs for energy, growth, and repair, it can break any food down into essential elements, and it does its job more skillfully than the most expert chemist. Flavor, odor, and texture are nothing more than the lures it uses to get you to put the food through its entrance—the opening in the body known as the mouth.

FOOD
AS FEELING

Your mind is an altogether different and more complicated "eater." Whereas the body seeks fuel in food and therefore breaks it down into simpler parts, the mind primarily seeks pleasure, comfort, or security in food. For this reason, the human senses and imagination often build food into something with complicated features and fantastic meanings. For your mind, a piece of chocolate layer cake is something more than sugar, starches, fats, and some vitamins and minerals. For your mind, whose ideas are fed by your senses, chocolate layer cake has a special odor, flavor, and texture. A legion of adjectives may be associated with the experience of eating chocolate cake: creamy . . . sweet . . . moist . . . fluffy . . . rich . . . luscious. And all of these special sensory descriptions have the power to prod memory and release a flood of emotions.

What do you think about when you picture a piece of chocolate layer cake? Perhaps you remember its odor and taste, and your mouth automatically begins to salivate in eager anticipation. You may associate it with a happy time—when it was served on your birthday, at a wedding, or on a date. Or it may call up not-so-happy memories—when you were alone and feeling down. You may not really have been hungry, but you gobbled up the cake anyway to ease your boredom or depression.

When your feelings, memories, and ideas about food lead you to take in the kinds and amounts of nutrients your body needs, then the two eaters within you are in harmony. But when emotions and ideas refuse the body necessary nutrients or force too much of them through its digestive system, the two eaters—body and mind—are at war with each other.

Emotional associations with food can be complex and contradictory. For some, food is a way to satisfy hunger as well as part of a way of life. A host of cultural customs involve the preparation, serving, and eating of food. Pleasure in food often takes center stage at festivities or special family occasions. For others, eating can be a dull, daily activity—a grudging acknowledgment of the body's dependence on its environment. For still others, the intense pleasures of eating seem hopelessly entangled with guilt. These people are ambivalent about food; their bodies and minds are at war with each other. And for this very reason, food often becomes a central concern in their lives, almost an obsession. Eating may be a pleasure they intensely seek. But the way they eat seems only to aggravate and escalate all of their negative feelings and problems. When conflicts escalate, food can become a serious addiction. Problem eating can become as controlling and as damaging as the abuse of drugs or alcohol.

EATING DISORDERS

Disagreements between the two kinds of "eaters" within us—the physical or biological "eater" and the psychological "eater"—are the cause of eating disorders. An eating disorder is any habit involving the intake or refusal of food that is detrimental to the body over the long haul.

Continually eating too much or too little are two kinds of behavior that could easily qualify as eating disorders. But these are not the only kinds of unhealthy eating habits. Others involve the *rhythm* of eating rather than the total amount of food consumed. Thus, a person who indulges in periodic food binges separated by periods of low intake of food may have an eating disorder—even though he or she does not take in too many calories per month or gain excess weight. Individuals who eat large amounts of food and then force their bodies to eliminate it by vomiting or by using laxatives are also suffering from an eating disorder.

You will learn all about the various kinds of eating disorders in the chapters that are to come. But here is a list of the three basic kinds:

1. *Compulsive overeating, or binge eating:* the practice of eating too much food or of not being able to stop eating. This practice sometimes focuses on or is triggered by a particular food. It may occur regularly or in "spells," in front of others or secretly. All obese people are not compulsive eaters, but about 40 percent of them are.

2. *Binging and purging, or bulimia nervosa:* the practice of eating large amounts of food and then eliminating them by forced vomiting or the use of laxatives or enemas. Bulimia may also include post-binge fasting or strict dieting, as well as strenuous exercise in an attempt to burn off calories.

3. *Self-starvation, or anorexia nervosa:* the practice of eating little or no food for extended periods of time. This disease is characterized by a body weight less than 85 percent of what is considered normal, an exaggerated fear of being fat, and (in females) the absence of three consecutive menstrual periods.[1]

Eating disorders may have existed since early times, but the study of eating disorders is a relatively recent science. In fact, problem eating was not recognized as a form of illness until about a hundred years ago, and it was not until about thirty years ago that it began to attract the attention of physicians, psychologists, and scientists. In the past fifteen years, we have entered a new era of awareness about eating disorders.[2] There has been a great increase in research and public awareness of these diseases. Nevertheless, the causes of eating disorders are still a matter for debate.

Professionals disagree even as to the field of science in which the study of eating disorders belongs. Biomedical researchers tend to stress the physiological causes of eating disorders and look for certain factors in brain chemistry, body metabolism, and heredity in their study of these diseases. On the other hand, psychiatrists, psychologists, psychotherapists, and self-help groups mostly focus on the emotions as the basis of problem eating. They try to uncover the cluster of ideas and feelings associated with the behavior, develop new ideas and feelings, and then work at making these a habit. At present, this latter approach has had the most practical success. This is due largely to the fact that researchers still know too little about the brain chemistry and metabolic processes involved in eating. This book will look at eating disorders predominantly from a psychological point of view, but some of the current research on the physiological causes of eating disorders also will be explained.

TOWARD A PSYCHOLOGY OF EATING DISORDERS

If people did not eat when they were not hungry or did not starve themselves when their bodies were crying out for nutrients, no one would have studied eating behavior. But over the years, certain similarities in the behavior of people with eating disorders have led psychiatrists and psychologists to come up with some basic assumptions about the psychology of most cases of problem eating.

The majority of experts believe that attitudes about eating and associations with specific foods are learned early in life. According to them, this is the reason feelings and behavior about eating sometimes seem to come from an unknown, seemingly uncontrollable source.

Food emotions are learned so early in life that, by the time we are old enough to notice them and think about them, we are no longer fully conscious of them. Incidents that shaped our eating attitudes go back farther than our first verbal experiences—to a time when we were being fed by breast or bottle.

What is more, early associations with food and eating may not affect a person until many years later, in adolescence or early adulthood.[3] And by that time, a host of other experiences have also influenced eating habits.

Most psychologists agree that for those who eat too much, too little, or in the wrong way, eating has become a way to handle unmanageable feelings. In this way, it serves the same purpose that abuse of alcohol or drugs serves for some people.[4] The absorbing, primal experience of tasting, chewing, and swallowing food can distract a person from anxious thoughts and soothe depression. It is an escape into a temporary feeling of security and calm. Eating quells negative emotions in the same way that putting a bottle or pacifier into a baby's mouth leads to an instantaneous end of the baby's tears.

However, negative eating is not only a remedy for but an expression of negative feelings. In almost every case, the expression of these negative feelings is indirect. Many problem eaters eventually learn that they have been filled with long-term rage without ever being aware of it. The effect their unhealthy eating had on others and on themselves was often an indirect expression of that intense anger. And at least partially, the anger had been turned inward toward self-punishment.

The mother of one fourteen-year-old girl who suffered from obsessive overeating and was severely overweight once wrote the following about her daughter in her diary: "T. eats so much, so fast, and in such large bites that it's almost as if she's trying to keep herself from throwing it at me." And indeed, as her daughter received therapy for her obsessive overeating, she slowly began to achieve an awareness of her buried resentments toward her mother.

In addition to anger, low self-esteem is at the root of many eating disorders. Although low self-esteem is self-perpetuating, one originally learns to devalue oneself as the result of a disheartening experience or situation. Low self-esteem may stem from thoughtless treatment by another family member and the inability to admit anger about that treatment; it may come from discouraging experiences in school; or it may be a response to messages in the culture at large.

Eating disorders can afflict anyone, but they are more prevalent among certain groups. For example, a high percentage of people with eating disorders are often found in sports or other activities that call for strict maintenance of body weight. Wrestlers, divers, long-distance runners, gymnasts, and ballet dancers sometimes develop an obsession with their body weight and shape that grows into an eating disorder.

Females comprise the majority of the population who suffer from eating disorders. Perhaps not coincidentally, they are also the object of most cultural messages about the human body. These messages are prescriptions for the "ideal" feminine body and the accepted standards of feminine beauty. Those who think they cannot measure up to this standard often suffer from low self-esteem. The next chapter examines some of our culture's ideal body images and shows how they may play a part in creating low self-esteem in some individuals—a prerequisite for most kinds of eating disorders.

Setting the Stage for an Eating Disorder

THE REAL BODY VERSUS IDEAL BODY IMAGES

One of the greatest influences on eating styles in our culture has been body image. Images are ideal pictures that spring from the creative imagination. And in this era of increased communications, millions of imaginations are now fed by all kinds of outside sources.

BODY IMAGE AND THE MEDIA

Turn on television. It won't take you long to decode the messages being sent out about ideal bodies. Whether it's Suzanne Sommers advertising a new thigh-thinning gadget or Rosanne Barr darkly deriding her own inability to lose weight, one thing becomes clear. America in the nineties has a fairly rigid and nearly uniform picture of the ideal feminine body.

Some of Janet Jackson's fans might still remember an energetic teenager with a sparkling smile and a rounded, voluptuous body. Fairly large-breasted, with ample buttocks and thighs, Janet Jackson definitely projected a different image from that of her rail-thin brother in her early rock videos—despite the similarities in their features, dancing styles, clothing, and music. But as she moved toward superstar status, something about her began to change. Janet got thinner. Her roundness was de-emphasized. In a sense, Janet Jackson was remodeled to more closely fit the nineties ideal of feminine beauty.

For women, the nineties ideal stresses health, active living, athletics, and sexuality. Magazines like *Self*, *New Woman*, and *Cosmopolitan* go on and on about the importance of the well-cultivated female body. Exercises for firming tummy, hips, and thighs; strategies for tightening the skin and getting rid of wrinkles; and clothing to show off the body's most alluring features are pretty much the same in all of these publications. All promote a belief in actively working to change and improve the body. The promise they hold out is that anyone who gives the right amount of attention to health, exercise, and skin-care strategies will attain the ideal form of thin thighs, firm bust, and glowing skin.

In many ways, today's woman is supposed to have a "manufactured" body. In other words, it is a body corrected and rebuilt by the right diets and exercises. Even surgical procedures, such as fat suction and breast implants, have become common. From this fact alone, it should be evident that the new body image—as healthy and as natural as it may seem—is about an *image* of health and nature rather than about these entities themselves.

BEAUTY'S BODY OVER TIME

Is there something inherently superior about thin thighs and a firm bust? A look at some of the ideal body images of other eras sheds some doubt on the absolute universality of the current ideal. The ideal American figure of the second half of the nineteenth century was in dramatic contrast to today's. It would even be considered grotesque by contemporary standards.

In 1850, the roundness ideal for women far exceeded the curves of Janet Jackson before her weight loss. A woman's "hour-glass" figure—about 36-25-38—was attained by lacing a body that we would consider overweight into a whalebone corset. This corset was fastened so tightly at the waist that over the years it sometimes created changes in the placement and shape of the woman's inner organs.[1] Even so, many doctors recommended it as being good for a woman's health because it aided posture. And perhaps they were right, because the ideal woman of the nineteenth century needed to carry a lot of fatty tissue on hips, buttocks, and breasts to achieve a successful hour-glass figure. Carrying around so much excess fatty tissue would lead to lower back problems for some.

By World War I, the French designer Coco Chanel had boldly liberated women from corsets. The new dresses were loose at the waist and hid the lines of the body. The ideal female body was thinner, as well. But during the 1920s, this trend led to other demands on the female body. Now big breasts and hips were completely out. Those who weren't flat-chested enough were actually encouraged to bind their breasts.

The new woman of the twenties had a lot in common with our woman of the nineties. She was supposed to be active and daring and healthy and self-reliant. In many cases she was entering the world of business for the first time. Perhaps for this reason, her body was streamlined into a boyish, less sexualized image.

Twenty years later, during World War II, women would enter the work force in much larger numbers. They often found themselves doing manual labor that had once been considered fit only for a man. It may be no coincidence that shoulder pads for women came into vogue at that time. This broadening of the shoulders gave women a sturdier, more masculine look that bordered on the military. Platform shoes, which made women look taller, became immensely popular.

By the 1950s, breasts and hips were back. The ideal feminine body ballooned like a float at the Macy's Thanksgiving Day parade. This new idea of women's bodies was not merely voluptuous but supervoluptuous. The overblown proportions of such actresses as Marilyn Monroe and Jane Russell were exaggerated by tight sweaters, uplift bras, and tapered skirts. The female body of the fifties stressed a woman's natural endowments. Yet few people in the fifties believed that exercise was an essential component of the healthy female body.

Then another change occurred. In the fashion industry, designers and photographers hypothesized that the rounded body distracted from the lines of the clothing that the model was supposed to advertise. The rail-thin model of the sixties, typified by Twiggy, became the norm. And that body type became the standard of feminine form.

Men's ideal body image has undergone changes over the years as well, though not nearly as dramatically. Formerly, a man was considered presentable as long as he fell within a certain median range of height and weight. But in recent years, men's bodies have tended to be looked at as raw material for a manufacturing process that takes place in the gym. The male body sculpted by weights and exercise and even in occasional cases by steroids or surgery is gaining popularity and will probably become the standard.

Does this constant fickleness in defining the ideal body mean that ideal body images are meaningless? Not really. Like every other human representation, body images are both an adaptation to and a comment on what is happening at the time. They reflect our attitudes toward nature, motherhood, sexuality, family, love, work, and other major components of our society.

Some elements of a particular body image are the result of fantasy. For example, the popularity of big-breasted women during the fifties may have been connected to the need for consolation—mothering—after the traumas of World War II. In other words, men were fantasizing a return to mother and an infantile state. Even the emphasis on the healthful-looking body of the nineties probably involves some fantasy. It answers a growing anxiety about pollution of the planet and the general threat to human health. It takes our minds off these seemingly insurmountable issues.

In some ways, body images are a sane, helpful response of a culture to changing conditions and new information. Liberating women from the corset was necessary at the beginning of the twentieth century so that women could move more freely as the range of their activities increased. And the active, athletic body of the nineties is at least a partial response to recent scientific discoveries about the value of exercise for both sexes in preventing heart disease and relieving stress. Thus, just like the act of eating, body images are an edgy alliance between two forces: the real demands of nature and our fantasies about it.

IS THERE
A TRULY
NORMAL BODY?

Whether body images are positive or negative, healthy or unhealthy is one thing to consider. But even if you are convinced that a particular body image is a sane, healthful one, you may not be able to conform to it.

The study of genetics has proved that inheritance plays a role in determining body size and shape. Weight, patterns of fatty deposits, and metabolism of food are all partly determined by family genes. If one of your parents is on the chubby side, you have about a 50 percent chance of becoming chubby as well. And if both are on the heavy side, your chance rises to 80 percent.[2]

Experts are divided as to how to interpret these statistics. Some claim that heavy parents tend to have heavy children because their children learn eating habits from them. But others cite numerous studies of twins separated at birth who maintain almost identical weights. This is evidence that inheritance plays a very central role in a person's body weight.

Aside from inheritance, there are other largely uncontrollable factors that can predispose a person to become heavy. For example, studies have shown that even thin mothers who gain a lot of weight in pregnancy are more likely to produce heavy babies. This suggests that a tendency to heaviness is at least in part established even before an individual is born.[3]

Even more specifically, some studies have found that different kinds of fatness are inherited by boys and by girls. In females, fatness or thinness of limbs tends to be an inheritable trait. But in males, only the amount of fat on the trunk seems to be inheritable.[4]

If limb slimness or fatness is determined by inheritance in girls, then the ideal of slim thighs would not always be a natural or logical ideal for some. A woman might be able to achieve slim thighs by enough exercise, starvation, or plastic surgery, but she might be working against her own natural body type.

After all this, you may now be wondering how a person can judge the fitness of her or his body without some standard against which to measure it. We may not need rigid stereotypes of ideal bodies, but each individual needs some kind of image on which to focus goals for health and well-being. The most obvious standard, of course, is a medical one. If your body has strength and flexibility and is free from diseases, then you are maintaining it properly.

In the past, another standard of body normalcy that allows for healthy variations was proposed. In the nineteenth century, a scientist named W. H. Sheldon came up with three main normal body types. His system of classification took into account muscle thickness and muscle tone, size of digestive cavities, bone thickness, and body profile. According to him, there were three different body types in the human species: the *ectomorph*, the *mesomorph*, and the *endomorph*. Ectomorphs are slender and light-boned; mesomorphs are stocky and muscular; and endomorphs are heavy and rounded.

Sheldon also built a theory of temperament around his three body types. His attribution of personality characteristics to the body types has since been disproved, but perhaps these types still can serve as a model for the normal physical self. If so, a mesomorph—a woman who has sturdy bones and tends to develop a lot of muscle tissue—might stop striving futilely for the delicate-boned look of the ectomorphic fashion model. And ectomorphs might abandon the impossible ideal of big breasts and rounded hips, contenting themselves instead with a slighter body.

Perhaps in the end, the best standard against which to judge one's body should be not weight or size but the proportion of fat in the body. This can be determined using a method called *densitometry.* Densitometry involves immersing the body in water. Then, when the weight of the body is divided by the volume of water displaced by it, the weight per unit of volume is obtained. Since fat is almost water-free and muscle contains a great deal of water, fat is less dense than muscle. A person with a lot of body fat will have a low body density and could be considered as not meeting the standards for a normal, healthy body. A person with less body fat will have a higher body density, and that person could be considered normal and healthy regardless of weight or size.

It should be kept in mind, however, that even such objective measurements have to be seen in the context of other factors. Normal percentages of body fat vary, depending on age and the particular processes happening inside the body. As an example, the bodies of girls generally change from about 15 percent body fat to 18 percent body fat as they enter adolescence and begin to menstruate.

BODY IMAGE AND EATING DISORDERS

It should now be clearer to you how reliance on culturally ideal body images can contribute to eating disorders. Trouble occurs when an idea, or fantasy, of what we should look like conflicts too dramatically with our actual bodies. Trying to conform to a strict body image can lead to self-starvation or overexercise. But perhaps even more dangerously, dissatisfaction with one's body because it falls short of a fantasy ideal can cause low self-esteem.

Many people with eating disorders have a hatred of their own bodies. What is wrong with their bodies may be apparent only to themselves, but this does not make the hatred any less intense or less damaging. They sometimes begin to believe that all of their problems would be solved if they could only lose a certain amount of weight. The weight becomes the focus, rather than the underlying problems the person is experiencing at home, with friends, or in school.

No one who dislikes her or his body takes good care of it. She or he may starve it, force it into uncomfortable clothing, or exercise it past the point of fatigue. Or that person may, conversely, take *too* good care of the body—just as a mother who is worried that her child might not be normal becomes obsessively overattentive and overconcerned. People who take too good care of their bodies are self-conscious about their appearance, obsessed with examining or caring for their bodies, or constantly worrying about health.

In another scenario, hatred of the body can lead to the desire to abuse it—to make it fatter because it will never be any thinner or to make it full and nauseous as a punishment for not meeting the goals that have been imposed on it. It is true that some very disciplined people who hate their bodies manage to suppress the tendency to abuse them. But this does not really represent an improvement in managing a low body self-image. The struggle against body hatred often leads to unmanageable stress, and anxiety and tension will work against the body regardless of the resolve of the most disciplined person.

Proof that body concerns lead to eating disorders lies in the fact that eating disorders are prevalent in certain professions where the body takes precedence. Actresses, models, and ballet dancers, all of whom must maintain very strict weights, sometimes end up with eating disorders. These disorders are not merely the unfortunate result of practical measures to protect a career, but rather the expression of deep and painful conflicts about the body's self-image.

You may be surprised to learn that many athletes are also prone to eating disorders. This has become such a problem in the sports world that both the American Medical Association and the American College of Sports Medicine have gone on record against the use of drastic weight-loss measures for athletes.[5] But eating disorders are not just a problem in professional sports. They also occur among high school wrestlers, runners, divers, and swimmers. Again, as in the case of actresses and dancers, eating disorders among athletes are not merely the result of going overboard in trying to meet the physical demands of a sport but are an emotionally unhealthy response to some of the values of that sport and its expectations for the body.

Eating disorders are always an inappropriate and self-defeating response to a problematic situation. They are never a good adjustment to it. In the next chapter, you will see how certain unproductive emotional reactions to a variety of problems can set up a person for the development of an eating disorder. In some of these descriptions, you may discover people you know, or you may even sense some facet of yourself.

The Eating Disorder Personality

WHEN FOOD TURNS AGAINST YOU

In a book titled *Anorexia, Bulimia, and Compulsive Overeating*, Kathleen Zraly, coordinator of the Eating Disorder Program at a New York State hospital, suggests changing the term "eating disorder" to "feeding disorder" because of the "inability of the eating-disordered people to 'feed' themselves self-love, comfort, and positive strokes."[1] Although the eating disorder itself may be a relatively recent phenomenon in a person's life, this inability to nurture the self probably was established quite early.

Zraly and her co-author, Dr. David Swift, feel that the most common and most central emotion of a person suffering from an eating disorder is shame. Using the theories of the well-known psychologist Erik Erikson as a basis for their ideas, Zraly and Swift locate the origins of a deep sense of shame in very early childhood, at about the age of two. This shame comes about when a two-year-old child mistakenly takes the blame for negative experiences. Such experiences can include unjust punishment, parental overprotection, a lack of attention to needs on the part of parents, physical abuse, or sexual abuse.[2]

According to *New York Times* personal health writer Jane E. Brody, as many as half of the people who suffer from eating disorders were sexually abused as young children. Many also come from families in which one or both parents was an alcoholic and/or physically abusive.[3]

Of course, in reality, the child is not at fault for these negative experiences, but he or she unwittingly assumes responsibility for them. And the sense of shame that grows from this self-blaming leads to low self-esteem. Such children often fear rejection or even abandonment by parents and others because they see themselves as deeply unworthy or "bad."

Most of the symptoms of eating disorders do not appear until adolescence or early adulthood. Zraly and Swift offer an interesting answer to the question of why. Adolescence and early adulthood are the times when individuals first begin to separate from parents and to lead lives of their own. These are also the times when a person develops serious friendships or romantic attachments. Those who suffered from negative experiences as a child may find the challenge of being self-sufficient or being intimate with another person very anxiety-provoking. The rejection and self-blame a person felt early in life may resurface with a vengeance. Simply put, the person may lapse into the frightened child that he or she once was. When these feelings are coupled with unresolved resentments, the resulting confusion may find expression in an eating disorder.

Eating is a broadly expressive kind of behavior

that can be used to symbolize a whole host of emotions. At the same time that it symbolizes these emotions, it can squelch them, cater to them, or conceal them. The following sections describe some typical behaviors and feelings of many problem eaters.

OBSESSIVE-COMPULSIVE BEHAVIOR

Obsessive means a tendency to become preoccupied with a disturbing idea. *Compulsive* means being irresistibly drawn to something. Obsessive-compulsive behavior does not necessarily imply a wholly obsessive-compulsive personality; but even when it doesn't, it is a symptom of unresolved conflicts or fears.

Everyone exhibits some obsessive-compulsive behavior at times. Did you ever skip to school, careful not to step on sidewalk cracks as you inwardly chanted, "Step on a crack and break your mother's back"? Or perhaps you've locked a door, then felt you had to return several times to recheck whether it really was locked.

Repetitive actions, such as washing and rewashing one's hands; rituals, such as always climbing into bed on the same side and with the same knee first; and excessive interest in a certain idea, such as not being able to stop thinking about or examining a sore, are all obsessive-compulsive forms of behavior. Everyone engages in them at some time in life. In every case, they are an effort to inject a feeling of control into something that feels out of control.

When Lady Macbeth chants, "Out, damned spot," rubbing her hand over and over, she is referring to imagined blood on her hands and is trying to exercise some control over an overwhelming feeling of guilt for having participated in a murder. The person who examines and reexamines a sore long after the doctor has said it is nothing is hoping by gazing at the sore to gain some control over overwhelming feelings of anxiety about it.

Obsessive-compulsive behavior is a reminder of primitive humans' early belief in magic. Tribal rituals, like the rain dance, seek by repetitive, stylized behavior to exercise control over forces of nature and other things over which an individual has no personal control. Just like the tribal dancer hopes to make it rain by certain repetitive body movements, the obsessive hand washer hopes to eliminate an unexplained and overwhelming feeling of being dirty by repeating the action of washing.

Most victims of the three major types of eating disorders are acting in an obsessive-compulsive manner. As an example, Jane Brody reports that most victims of anorexia nervosa (self-starvation) have an exaggerated fear of weight gain. They are overcritical of their bodies and preoccupied with becoming unrealistically thin. They may weigh themselves several times a day, shifting from ecstasy to dismay each time the needle moves down or up by a hair's breadth.[4] They may study themselves in a mirror ten to twenty times per hour. Some meticulously and ritualistically plan every detail of an extremely low-calorie meal, eat the same food at the same time every day, or cut food into tiny, perfectly arranged pieces before eating. Still others spend an enormous amount of time preparing delicious food but will serve it only to family or guests and refuse to eat it themselves.

Most binge eaters (compulsive overeaters) cannot stop or control the kinds of food they eat. They are obsessed with a certain food and feel compelled to eat massive amounts of it whenever they come across it. They cannot, for example, pass a bakery without buying and devouring six of their favorite cookies.

Self-starvers, or bulimics (bingers and purgers), are sometimes obsessed with a fantasy of health, questioning at all times whether the food put into their body meets the strictest standards. These people resemble obsessive hand washers in their struggle to escape an inner sense of pollution or shame. But in every case, these people are hoping that their behavior will magically keep a particular cluster of negative feelings in check.

What are these feelings? In most cases the person experiencing them cannot voice them because he or she does not understand them. That is why they seem out of control. As was stated before, many theorists maintain that the feelings the person with an eating disorder is trying to control stem from negative, largely unremembered childhood experiences. Although it is difficult to generalize for all of those who have eating disorders, two eating disorder specialists, Denise M. Montero and Dodi C. Ardalan, have created broad categories meant to summarize the most common feelings.[5] They have also reported the most common statements made by sufferers of eating disorders that are expressive of these feelings. Some typical feelings and statements of people with eating disorders are presented and discussed below. Keep in mind as you read them that they are not completely distinct from each other but flow together in constantly shifting emotional patterns.

Control

For compulsive overeaters, binge eaters, or bulimics, the issue of being or not being in control is crucial. Being in complete control is the desired goal. Any hint of missing this goal activates their low self-esteem and makes them feel that they are "bad." It reminds them of a time in early childhood when they "let go" and were punished for it.

People who are obsessed with being in control get unbearably distressed when they do the slightest thing that does not show control. At that point they often "throw the towel in" and let go completely.

Afterward they become filled with shame and remorse and make a solemn vow never to lose control again. But at the slightest sign of weakness, they become so disgusted with themselves that they let go again. The cycle continues, and each round brings self-esteem down another notch.

Thus, according to this model, a compulsive overeater, who is likely to be obsessed with control, might set up "too perfect" eating plans for herself. As soon as she fails to meet the unreasonable demands of such a diet, she will probably let go and fall into a desperate binge. Since such a person feels ashamed, she will probably eat the forbidden food quickly and secretly, to dispose of the food so that the binge will not happen again. Then she will make the terms of her diet even more stringent as a punishment for her lapse. The stricter diet will cause another lapse, and the cycle will begin again.

If the person is bulimic, she may try to reverse the "damage" by vomiting the food that should not have been eaten. All and all, the compulsive overeater and the bulimic slip in and out of control continually and never find a happy medium.

Some typical attitudes:[6]

"How could I have done this to myself?"

"I am all bad."

"Tomorrow I will get back on the diet."

"I am lacking or am not entitled to make mistakes or feel this anger."

The Need for Approval and Dependency
Montero and Ardalan maintain that many people with an eating disorder were given the message that they must achieve perfection to get their parents' approval. Their parents may have been highly critical of themselves or of their children, both of which

lead to the setting up of this impossible standard. Thus, the person with an eating disorder feels that he or she needs to behave according to an exact formula to feel loved or to get approval. Such people are often highly dependent on their parents. Self-esteem becomes a question of doing what others want.

In such cases, eating can fulfill two needs. Since the person bases all good feelings on the approval of others, when this approval is not forthcoming, the person feels empty and without identity. Food erases the feeling of being empty and unloved. As Montero and Ardalan write, "Food symbolically is a way to 'connect' with the self, the substance within; a way to take care of the self's needs and 'fill up the emptiness.' " In search of this "food," the person may become a compulsive overeater.

The second need that the food satisfies is the need to *rebel* against being dependent on others. A person with an eating disorder resents his or her need for others. In rebellion against it, he or she may eat indiscriminately because the eating is at least something that is not under others' control. Conversely, he or she may refuse to eat and become anorexic because saying no is also a way of defying others' control.

Some typical attitudes:

"I do not know how to define myself and meet my own needs."

"I feel empty and behave so as to obtain approval from others."

"I resent my dependence and eat."

Rejection of Others
As much as a person with an eating disorder needs the approval of others, he or she also rejects all

others. In a sense, problem eaters do not know how to establish boundaries. They either feel totally dependent or "don't need anybody at all." In this sense, problem eaters don't know how to be separate persons. Their image of themselves is always related to people outside themselves.

Eating suppresses the feeling of dependence on others and provides a buffer against the outside world. It becomes a substitute for relating to others or feeling vulnerable to them. When a binge eater fears the rejection of others, he or she retreats into eating. Food becomes a protective mechanism.

Some typical attitudes:

"I must try to take care of myself by eating because I cannot ask from others what I need."

"He or she does not like me because I'm fat."

"When I am fat, I feel protected, docile, all-giving, nonvulnerable, nonsexual."

THE ANGRY EATER[7]

In all three major types of eating disorders (binge eating, bulimia, and self-starvation), the emotions and attitudes described above blend together to produce several distinct personality characteristics associated with problem eating. One of the most common of these personality characteristics is *anger*.

Most therapists who deal with eating disorders agree that more patients fit into the angry-eater personality category than any other. And few of these angry eaters are even aware that they are angry.

In many cases, the emotions of the angry eater stem from that period in childhood when a person learns to be independent. Very young infants are completely dependent upon their mothers for almost everything—food, protection, waste disposal, and moving about. But as a child learns to pick up and eat food himself, to control his own bowel movements, and to get about alone, he or she enters a new stage of development. For the first time, he or she begins to realize a separation between the self and others.

At this time, a child experiments with self-assertiveness, anger, and rejection of others. He or she may throw food or toys, hit, or make loud, disruptive sounds. Such behavior is a way of testing boundaries, a way of experimentally rebelling from the old dependency. All children go through it. However, if parents or others disapprove too strongly of such behavior, or if a parent's own angry behavior is of a violent nature, the child may learn to feel fear and shame about assertiveness and anger. He or she may repress angry feelings because they have been labeled as unacceptable or dangerous.

The above should make it clear to you that the anger of such a person is never expressed directly. Such a person is dealing with years of pent-up feelings that only dare to come out in coded, largely self-defeating ways. Angry eaters learned early in life that independent behavior can be dangerous or can arouse disapproval in others. Consequently, the angry eater is still inwardly very dependent on the approval of others.

The angry eater also feels alienated. Because such a person feels that negative feelings will never be accepted, the deep down belief is that he or she will be experienced as "bad." Such a person wants no part of the outside world and the feelings it provokes. Since food comes from the outside world, the angry person often feels disgust for it.

For angry eaters, the experience of eating may be reminiscent of the time anger had to be "swallowed." Such a time may actually have occurred.

For example, a child may have been forced over and over again to eat a food that was not appealing. The child may have wanted to throw the food across the room and been punished for trying to. Not only did the food have to be swallowed but the feeling of disgust and anger associated with the food had to be "swallowed" as well. A person who associates food with "swallowing anger" often eats rapidly in big, largely unchewed gulps. This characteristic is true of many binge eaters. Such eating is a way of rejecting the food one was prevented from rejecting and is often a way of expressing the anger itself as well. Angry eaters often like to binge on crunchy, salty food such as corn chips, nuts, and crackers. The gnashing of their teeth and the sounds of the food being crushed are in part an expression of the anger they feel.

Binge eating also shuts off emotions. As long as the person keeps eating, he or she does not have to confront anger. Too much food acts as a depressant that slows down bodily sensations and blunts feelings. The eating produces a layer of fat, which distances others and expresses the angry eater's alienation. It may also have the added benefit of getting "revenge" on others when they start to worry about the angry eater's health or appearance.

For a person who is a binge eater, weight reduction can be highly threatening. According to two eating disorder theorists, Jonathan Kurland Wise, M.D., and Susan Kierr Wise, "The fear of too much weight loss is the fear that the true inner self—full of anger—will be exposed. . . . Therefore, over-compensatory behavior keeps it in check: this type of patient appears to the outside world as a low-keyed, nonaggressive, nice guy. He is living a lie and deep down he knows it. . . . He cannot expose himself by shedding his fat."[8]

The Wises have found that a large percentage of binge eaters had alcoholic parents.[9] Such parents were often the cause of frightening episodes of rage or disorder in the home. When the child witnessed these, he or she began to fear the consequences of angry feelings. In addition, such children have learned that they cannot look to their parents for help in mastering or controlling negative feelings. Consequently, these feelings become shrouded in fear and shame. The individual becomes someone terribly afraid to lose control.

In her book *The Yo-Yo Syndrome Diet*, psychotherapist Doreen L. Virtue maintains that women often have difficulty experiencing and expressing anger.[10] She traces this tendency to social pressures, ranging from parents' teachings to the expectations for women in the work place. Adolescents also often have trouble expressing or mastering anger. Consequently, their eating habits can be highly erratic— they are often influenced by an instinct for rebellion that might suddenly be interrupted by feelings of dependency and fear of acting on their own. You will read more about adolescent eating patterns below.

THE DEPRESSED EATER

Many angry eaters are also depressed. Depression is characterized by a lack of energy, a lingering sadness, and a loss of ambition. If the depression is serious and lasts long enough, it can eventually result in near-total paralysis.

Inability to accept strong emotions such as anger often leads to depression because it creates a sensation of emptiness and a lack of identity. Deep depression is always accompanied by low self-esteem.

Different people have different ways of coping with depression. Because depression instills one with a sense of listlessness and inactivity, some sufferers decrease intake of food or even stop eating altogether. After all, eating does require some activity and initiative. Such people may become self-starvers. Others may stuff themselves when they are depressed. Afraid to express their turbulent feelings, they choose instead to punish themselves. This stuffing behavior merely escalates the depression because it does not lead to a true expression of the denied anger. Eating too much then results in disappointment and a gnawing sense of being unfulfilled.

Many depressed people overeat as a way of combating the feelings of fatigue caused by depression.[11] Hoping to curtail the listlessness and inertia that are the symptoms of depression, they unconsciously choose quick-energy foods that are high in sugar. Though these foods may give them a small, short-term lift, the consequent letdown usually increases the depressed feeling.

Doreen Virtue has noticed that people who are chronically depressed often overindulge in dairy products, such as ice cream and cheese. She claims that the overeater intuitively focuses on these foods because some of the proteins in dairy foods have the same effect on the brain as antidepressant medication.[12] Other depressed eaters concentrate on chocolate. Virtue cites studies showing that chocolate contains a chemical similar to a substance produced in the brain when a person is in love. It is a possibility that depressed people eat chocolate in an attempt to reproduce this "romantic high."

Often a person who claims to be eating out of simple boredom is really depressed. As was explained, depression is sometimes a result of being out of touch with stronger, more negative feelings such as anger. Being out of touch with feelings makes a person feel hollow or empty. This feeling is often associated with being "bored."

THE AMBIVALENT EATER

Every type of problem eater is plagued by ambivalence. *Ambivalence* is a simultaneous attraction to and repulsion from something. Problem eaters are ambivalent about their bodies: they dislike them, but they are obsessed with them. They are ambivalent about the act of eating: they need food desperately, but they hate that need. And they are also ambivalent about the outside world.

Zraly and Swift point out that "eating is one of the most primitive means by which people take in something from their environment and make it part of themselves." From this they conclude that eating disorders express an ambivalence about "taking in something that the world is offering; something the individual needs and wants, but also dislikes and fears."[13]

Zraly and Swift, as well as other eating disorder theorists, also maintain that the "something" both needed and feared is intimacy—stemming originally from feelings of intimacy about parents or other care givers. Thus, a person with an eating disorder feels dependent and craves intimacy. Yet negative experiences surrounding intimacy—usually from early years and involving parents—have made her or him distrustful of it.

Problem eaters' conflicts with food are a way of expressing their conflicts about intimacy and nurturing. They both need and fear these behaviors. Consider the binge eater. During certain periods that person rejects the need for the nurturing comforts of food. Then, suddenly, the need comes pouring out in an uncontrollable way. The person gives in to the need for nurturing and takes it in in huge gulps that express deep deprivation. Such a person is ambivalent, not only about food but about human closeness and trust.

THE
ADOLESCENT
EATER

For most problem eaters, ambivalence about intimacy—and consequently, ambivalence about food—is first experienced during adolescence. As stated before, adolescence is the time in a person's life when the first major shift away from parents and home occurs. In a way, the adolescent is like the two-year-old child first learning to move about and to eat by herself. And because of this new stage of independence, conflicts about dependency begin to resurface.

It is a known and accepted fact that small children naturally go on food binges. Many refuse to eat anything or will eat only a favorite food for days on end, then suddenly begin consuming large quantities. This is their way of exploring the outside world and the pleasures of eating. But it's also their way of rebelling and asserting their independence.

In the same way, teenagers are preoccupied with asserting their independence and establishing an identity that is truly theirs. To do this they must, at least temporarily, reject some of the intimacy and identification they feel with their parents. During this time, they may rebel. One way to rebel is to reject the parents' model of "sensible" eating. Just to show that they are their "own person," teenagers may refuse to eat the regular meals or the balanced diet for which their parents are pleading. This behavior may be misinterpreted by parents, and the resultant friction is likely to compel the teenager to rebel even more against parental control.

However, just the opposite may occur during the teenage years. Instead of rebelling directly, the teenage eater may collapse under the pressure of over-bearing parents. As a dramatic expression of inability to achieve a feeling of independence, the teenager may become a slothful "couch potato"—a kind of passive "nonentity" whose only assertiveness lies in defiant munching. The bonus from this kind of passive behavior is that it may upset the parents—getting their needed attention and at the same time expressing a refusal to do what they want.

Some forms of teenage ambivalence and rebellion can take on dangerous dimensions. In anorexia, which you will read about in detail later, a teenager may reject food so completely that he or she risks death by starvation. Eating disorder theorists have suggested that when a teenage girl expresses such complete rejection of food, she may be rejecting identification with her mother's body. Such a girl does not want the womanly hips, thighs, and breasts of her mother and other mature women. She feels overcontrolled by her mother and does not want to identify with her in any way. At the same time, she fears growing up and eventually leaving home. The development of a woman's adult body is just too threatening.[14]

In this chapter, you have seen how a complex web of often contradictory emotions can be acted out in the arena of eating. At present, most physicians and psychotherapists who treat eating disorders and/or obesity approach these diseases from a psychological angle. However, data suggesting some biochemical bases for obesity and problem eating have recently come to light.

Eating Disorders and Being Fat

IS THERE A BIOLOGICAL CAUSE?

Now that you understand some of the psychological causes of eating disorders, it's time to take a look at some possible physiological causes. Lately, theories about these causes have been garnering more and more attention among professionals and in the popular press.

Any responsible therapist or physician whose job is the treatment of eating disorders and weight problems will not automatically rule out a biological cause when a patient first comes seeking help. If the professional suspects a physiological cause for obesity, excessive thinness, or abnormal eating patterns, the patient may first be referred to an *endocrinologist,* a physician who specializes in the diagnosis and treatment of glandular diseases. In a small number of cases, problem eating, obesity, or excessive thinness actually is caused by a malfunctioning gland.

In evaluating a patient, an endocrinologist first obtains a complete medical history. The medical history may then lead to a hypothesis about a glandular disorder. And that hypothesis will be confirmed or disproved by a series of laboratory tests.

An example of a glandular disease that can lead to an eating disorder or weight problem is thyroid disease. An overactive or underactive thyroid can produce abnormal eating behavior as well as weight gain or weight loss. Even though only a fraction of eating disorders or weight problems seem to be the result of thyroid disease or other glandular problems, this does not mean that there is absolutely no physical basis to problem eating or weight abnormalities.

NEW EVIDENCE ABOUT OBESITY AND OVEREATING

In February 1988, the *New York Times* ran an article on its front page about two new studies of obesity. Until that time, most obese persons were thought to be suffering from eating disorders. The theory was simple. People got obese because they ate too much, and they ate too much for psychological reasons.

But here was a new theory that contradicted the old assumption, plainly spelled out in the headline: "New Obesity Studies Indicate Metabolism Is Often to Blame." On another page of the same edition of the *Times* was an even blunter headline. This one ran: " 'People Are Born to Be Fat.' "[1]

One of the reported studies, which had been published in *The New England Journal of Medicine* that day, had focused on Indians living in the Southwest. Scientists had chosen the Indians because 80 to 85 percent of this particular group—Pima Indians in Arizona—tended to become obese by their early twenties. To find out why, researchers kept track of how many calories ninety-five Pima Indian men and women, whose weights averaged 210 pounds (94.5 kg), burned in twenty-four-hour periods. They found that those who gained the most weight had bodies that burned fewer calories per hour. In other words, the weight gainers had slower metabolisms.

Researchers also discovered another surprising fact. It seemed that many obese people with average metabolisms suddenly "shifted gears" if they ever did manage to lose weight. When they got thinner, their metabolism slowed down, causing them to burn fewer calories and to gain back the weight they had lost.

On that same day, the *Times* also ran an article about a certain Dr. Jules Hirsch, a researcher at Rockefeller University Hospital in New York, who now felt vindicated by the new studies. For years Hirsch had been suggesting that people got fat because of biochemical or cellular differences in their bodies. The new studies supported his theories. But in the article Dr. Hirsch went further. He also said he believed that people who are obese are signaled by their bodies in some way that actually *forces them to eat,* which is why they find it so difficult to stop eating and get thin.

Dr. Hirsch does not believe that being obese is good for anyone. In an interview he stressed the medical dangers of being fat (heart disease, diabetes, and lower back problems), and he also counseled overweight people to work hard at losing weight. Nevertheless, his blaming of not only obesity but problem eating on biological causes shocked many because it brought the problem completely out of the realm of the psychological and into the realm of the physical.

Some scientists now believe that certain people are programmed by their genes to store calories instead of burning them. This tendency to store rather than burn increases as these people lose weight. A few have suggested that this characteristic may be a leftover trait from early humans, who had to live off body fat during long periods of famine. During these periods, the person who was able to slow down body metabolism was the one who survived.[2]

You may now be saying to yourself, "This is all well and good, but what practical advantage does this information offer to anyone who suffers from obesity or overeating?" At the moment, it offers very little advantage except to take the "blame" off people who cannot seem to lose as much weight as they want to—no matter how hard they try. Removing the blame for weight gain can do marvels for a person's self-esteem. It can, hopefully, lead to gradual weight loss through sane, healthy diets. And it can also discourage impossible expectations.

Sometime in the future, this research may have great clinical application as well. If scientists can learn to thoroughly understand the slow metabolism of those who gain weight, then they may be able to figure out a way to change it by administering drugs. However, such a possible approach to weight problems or eating disorders still lies in the uncertain future.

PROBLEM EATING, OBESITY, AND THE BRAIN[3]

At one time, eating and appetite were associated only with the stomach, but over the past century researchers have been trying to determine the relationships that exist between body weight, eating, and brain chemistry. Much of the research has stemmed from a discovery by a nineteenth-century physician named Frolich.

Dr. Frolich was intrigued by a patient whose weight had nearly doubled in a relatively short time. After the patient died, a large tumor was discovered near the base of his brain. The tumor had damaged the patient's hypothalamus, a gland instrumental in regulating the autonomic nervous system.

Further studies showed that damage to one part of the hypothalamus seemed to produce overeating and obesity in humans and other animals. Damage to another area of the hypothalamus seemed to produce the opposite effect—self-starvation. Many scientists surmised from this that a person overate or underate chronically only when one of these two parts was not functioning properly.

But this was only part of the picture. Eventually, researchers learned that damage to the first part of the hypothalamus did *not* produce overeating if the subject was *already* overweight. And damage to the other area of the hypothalamus did *not* produce self-starvation if the subject was *already* very thin. These discoveries suggested that both parts of the hypothalamus functioned together to maintain a certain *set point* of body weight.

A body *set point* is like a setting on a thermostat. A thermostat turns the heat on when the temperature falls below the set point and turns it off when the temperature rises above it, thus maintaining temperature within a narrow range. In the same way, the two parts of the hypothalamus may turn eating and calorie burning on and off to maintain body weight at a fixed set point. Once a person goes below an individual set point, his or her metabolism slows down, and appetite is stimulated. If the person goes above it, metabolism may speed up, and appetite will diminish.

According to this theory, people are the weight

they are because of a setting in their brain rather than because of psychological problems or bad behavior. The idea of the set point is far from universally accepted by experts in the field of eating disorders. But those who do accept it think that eating is controlled by body weight rather than the opposite. Such a point of view is a radical one. It suggests that fat must send some kind of signal to the hypothalamus that tells it when there is too much, too little, or just enough according to a predetermined, possibly inherited value. Some have suggested that the signal from fat travels through the blood to the brain as fat is utilized by body cells.

"BROWN FAT"

Could there be other reasons why some people seem to gain weight so much more easily than others do? For example, why is it that many teenagers can eat immense amounts of food without getting fat? Older people who eat the same amount and who are no more or no less active often seem to gain.

Researchers now suspect that different people utilize the same amount of calories in different ways. Only about 20 percent of the calories humans burn is used for voluntary activity.[4] Of the remaining 80 percent, some is used for involuntary activity—heartbeat, breathing, and brain activity—but a significant proportion of the calories is wasted. The calories are released from the body into the atmosphere as heat.

There is increasing evidence that some people get rid of more calories by producing more heat than others do. Overweight people seem to expend less energy this way. Instead of converting the food calories into heat, they tend to store them. Newborn infants and teenagers seem to release large amounts of food energy as heat. Consequently, they tend to gain less weight from eating large amounts of food.

The amount of heat energy a person produces may be related to that person's amount of *brown adipose tissue,* or *brown fat.* The only function of brown fat is to produce heat in the body. Brown fat is exceptionally efficient at this task. It is the kind of fat that is known to increase when the human body is constantly exposed to cold.

Bears use their brown fat to raise their body temperature as they come out of hibernation in the spring. And human babies have the ability to produce a lot of brown fat. As brown fat turns food energy into heat, it burns a lot of calories. Consequently, a person with a lot of brown fat could process large amounts of food without getting fat. The tendency to make brown fat declines markedly as a person nears thirty. This may be why older people tend to gain weight more easily.

OTHER POSSIBLE FACTORS

Brain chemistry and lack of brown fat are not the only suggested physical causes of eating disorders and obesity. In 1989, an article in *The New England Journal of Medicine*[5] discussed some metabolic diseases that resulted in defective *lipoprotein lipase* activity. Lipoprotein lipase is an enzyme produced by many tissues in the body. It is important in the metabolism of certain fats and fat proteins. People suffering from abnormal activity of this protein tended to become obese.

In 1991, another article in *The New England Journal of Medicine*[6] discussed the relationship between quitting smoking and gaining weight. Over nine thousand subjects were interviewed ten years after quitting smoking. It was found that the average permanent weight gain for those who stopped smoking was just over 6 pounds (2.7 kg) for men and over 8 pounds (3.6 kg) for women. Almost 10 percent of the men and over 13 percent of the women who had quit smoking had gained about 30 pounds (13.5 kg). Whether this weight gain was due to physiological causes has not been established.

In any case, as time passes, the evidence for physiological factors in eating behavior and in the gaining or loss of weight seems to be accumulating. Currently, there is not much anyone can do to control these factors. However, an awareness of them can work positively for someone with an eating disorder. Most obviously, it may serve as a voice of reason for those problem eaters who are obsessed with the issue of control. Perhaps these people should consider that their body might have a "mind" of its own, consisting of a natural set point for weight and mechanisms for burning calories. Their best bet might be to follow its cues and to stop trying to force it into ideal, perfectionist patterns. Evidence of physiological factors in eating and weight patterns are a sign to us that we cannot completely control our bodies.

The Diet Dilemma

Body set points and fat metabolism may be one reason the majority of diets simply do not work permanently. The statistics currently surrounding American dieting are grim. Less than 5 percent of those who diet manage to get slim or stay that way.[1]

Nevertheless, a high failure rate does not keep most Americans from dieting. A recent survey of California school-age females revealed that almost 90 percent of the seventeen-year-olds were dieting. Although 60 percent of these dieters claimed that they were dieting because they were overweight, the researchers found that only 20 percent could clinically be said to be above their normal weight![2]

Such statistics indicate that dieting is not a wholly rational activity for some people. Perhaps for this reason, diets that promise miracles or claim to possess special powers of weight loss can, at least briefly, achieve such popularity.

In the past forty years, a host of schemes for weight loss have taken the market by storm before people have become fully aware of their limitations. In the early 1960s, for example, a women's magazine promoted a "fat metabolism" diet that required the dieter to drink a glass of vegetable oil before the dinner meal! Needless to say, some people temporarily lost weight. They were so nauseated by the vegetable oil that they lost their appetite for dinner.

In the seventies and eighties, diets that promised quicker weight loss by the use of liquid protein, liquid shakes, "grapefruit pills," or high- or low-carbohydrate-content food were immensely popular and were promoted in books and magazine articles. People lost weight, at least temporarily, on many of them. But none have been proven to work any better than a simple reduction of calories.

Through the years, various diet aids have sought to diminish appetite by the use of substances that expand in the stomach, anesthetize the taste buds, or give the body a false sense of energy by speeding up heartbeat. Again, these substances may diminish intake of food temporarily, but since they never deal with retraining eating habits, the weight comes back in the majority of cases. What is more, the drugs in these remedies can themselves be dangerous to a person's health. Over-the-counter diet pills can be especially harmful. Almost all of them contain the same ingredients: a substance similar to a decongestant and caffeine. The accelerated heart rate and increase in blood pressure that results from taking the decongestant-like substance and the caffeine can damage a person's circulatory system.

THE HAZARDS OF DIETING[3]

Even those on sensible diets that do not pretend to be miracles face difficulties. Fat has a high-energy density and can only be burned off slowly. Worse is the fact that fat burning seems to slow down as a diet progresses.

For most people, the first week of dieting is an encouraging experience. An average of 4 to 5 pounds (1.8–2.2 kg) melts away as if it were water. It is. Most of the weight loss at the beginning of a diet results from water loss and loss of glycogen. It does not represent a loss in actual fat.

What is more, diets that significantly reduce calorie intake tend to give your body the message that it is being starved. Consequently, the body responds defensively. After a few days on a diet, the body cuts down energy loss through limiting its production of excess heat. Calories are now burned more slowly. At this point in a diet, a person stops losing weight temporarily or may even gain some—despite sticking religiously to a diet of as low as one thousand calories a day.

Even those who continue to lose weight do not always lose it from their fat deposits. They may use up deposits of glucose and glycogen in the liver, then in muscle cells, and then start burning muscle protein. The using up of muscle protein makes the dieter experience extreme weakness and fatigue.

Regardless of the diet, the majority of people gain back all of the weight they have lost within a year. And perhaps the greatest hazard of dieting is the psychological effects it produces in people who have failed. Although failing at a diet is the norm, failed dieters often sink into depression and into worse eating habits. They may increase the intake of fats and sugars in their diet and lose the morale for exercising. An obsession with dieting that is fraught with failure can be the prelude to any of the three major types of eating disorders.

YO-YO DIETING[4]

Despite the discouraging results for dieters, most failed dieters eventually try again. And again. Repeated, failed attempts at dieting are now known as *yo yo dieting*. Although the syndrome of constantly re-beginning dieting is not yet classified as an eating disorder, its effects can sometimes lead to one.

In 1987, researchers at the University of Pennsylvania Medical School began to pay specific attention to yo-yo dieting when a young woman they had put on a 420-calorie diet simply stopped losing weight. They discovered that the woman had dieted many times in her life before but had always gained her weight back.

In an effort to find out if repeated dieting had anything to do with the woman's inability to lose weight now, the researchers collaborated with a Vassar College biologist in a study of several groups of adult male rats. One group of rats was put on a high-fat diet and quickly became obese. The same group was then put on a balanced weight-loss diet and went back to their normal weight. Then they were offered high-fat food again, and they regained the extra weight. The cycle was then repeated.

On phase two of the cycle, the rats lost weight twice as slowly and put it on again three times faster. What was happening was that the rats were beginning to use the food more efficiently. They actually required fewer calories to get fat.

To confirm their results, the researchers began looking at humans who had lost and regained their weight. In the subjects they studied, weight loss was harder for a great majority the second time around. It was also discovered that yo-yo dieting could alter body tissue so that a higher percentage is composed of fat. Thus, a person may be the same weight before and after a dieting cycle, but the new weight will contain more fat that is harder to burn off.

There is even some evidence that yo-yo dieting can change food preferences. One study found that female rats preferred more fat in their diet once they had been through the dieting cycle.

Studies with wrestlers have confirmed the data on yo-yo dieting. College wrestlers frequently lose weight quickly before a match in order to compete in a class below their usual weight. After a match, they put the weight back on by eating more. Wrestlers who did this seemed to have a much lower resting metabolic rate than those who did not. Their ability to burn off calories and lose weight had decreased.

YO-YO DIETING AND EATING DISORDERS

The cyclical nature of yo-yo dieting represents a serious threat to the person at risk for an eating disorder. As you have learned, most people at risk for a eating disorder are concerned with control. The endless round of dieting, failing, and beginning again can make a person feel more and more out of control. And as the ability to burn calories decreases, self-esteem can drop.

A common practice of some yo-yo dieters on the weight-gain segment of the cycle is binging. Binge eaters rarely feel they want to eat. A compulsion drives them to do it. For most bingers, the practice is exaggerated by the dieting in-between. The most extreme binges come after a period of strict denial. Then hunger or frustration because the diet does not work causes a slip. The slip causes shame, which leads the dieter to let go completely and binge.

Binge eaters usually concentrate on a specific

kind of food. They are able to eat normally in a lot of cases, but when they come across this certain food or food group, uncontrolled eating eventually results. In her book *The Yo-Yo Syndrome Diet,* Doreen L. Virtue asks binge eaters to analyze their relationship to their particular binge food by asking themselves some questions about it:[5]

○ How does eating this food make me feel? Calm or energized, happy or depressed? What other emotions does it trigger in me?

○ Have I ever been able to eat just one piece or bite of this food? Do I want more the next day or later in the week?

○ When I eat this food, do I feel guilty or nervous afterward?

○ How many times have I begun an eating binge because I've tasted this food?

Virtue also describes some typical binge foods and surmises why they appeal to compulsive eaters. These foods include chocolate, other sweets, salty junk foods, dairy products, starchy foods, highly spiced foods, and even some "health" foods.

Chocolate is one of the most popular binge foods. It contains the stimulant caffeine as well as a chemical called phenylethylamine, the chemical that has been associated with romantic love. The aroma of chocolate also contains pyrazine, a chemical that has been known to activate pleasure centers in the brain when inhaled. It makes sense that chocolate would appeal to compulsive eaters since, as we have seen, many of them are concerned with issues of nurturing and emotional dependence.

Virtue points out that spicy Mexican and Italian foods, with their aged cheeses and yeasty crusts, contain a chemical called tyramine. Tyramine is a stimulant that elevates mood and gives a temporary energy boost. Virtue reasons that those who binge on spicy foods may be craving stimulation and excitement in their lives. Again, this hypothesis seems to make sense in light of the fact that many compulsive eaters must struggle with a sense of inner emptiness and numbness.

Since yo-yo dieting puts the individual on a roller coaster of weight loss and weight gain, as behavior it can serve as an expression of deep ambivalence. And a binger whose self-esteem is reduced at each increasingly downward curve becomes more and more ambivalent about the momentary comforts and disastrous letdowns of overeating. Perhaps because of this, some bingers eventually go on to *bulimia*. Bulimia is the practice of binging and purging. People afflicted with bulimia may eat massive amounts of food until the stomach feels as if it is bursting. Then they will make themselves vomit by a variety of means, or they may take laxatives in an effort to remove the now disgusting food as quickly as possible from their bodies.

Bulimia and anorexia, which is self-starving, may be the most dramatic expressions of conflicts about eating. You will learn more about the causes, habits, and hazards of these eating disorders in the next chapter. But before you go on to that chapter, consider what attitude you might need to take toward dieting if you are someone who really should lose weight.

MAKING THE BEST OF DIETING AND HEALTHY EATING

Since obesity can be responsible for serious health problems, it might be wise not to let discouraging statistics about the failure rate of dieting keep you from taking good care of your body. But rather than looking for rapid, dramatic results and novel dieting methods, it would be best to learn some long-term healthy eating habits.

If you are eating to lose weight, you will want to eat the *same way* that you will be eating after the weight loss. Foods eaten on a diet should not be any different from the foods one should eat daily to promote health and keep up growth and energy. The only difference is that if you are overweight, you might need to eat a little bit less of these foods, and combine the effort with exercise.

The hazards of a drastic reduction in calories are many and serious. As you have read, they include lowering your metabolic rate, losing morale, and falling into the yo-yo syndrome. In view of this, it makes more sense not to diet at all but merely to eat daily the amount of calories eaten by a person of your height and normal weight. As your body falls into harmony with this kind of eating, it will find its own natural weight. If eating what the average person of average weight eats is a *reduction* in food intake for you, you will probably lose weight. But if your eating rhythms are regular and the foods you choose are healthy and of reasonable portions, then whatever the results, you can be sure that you are doing the best you can for yourself and your body.

Dangerous Obsessions

ANOREXIA NERVOSA AND BULIMIA

When it comes to eating disorders, anorexia nervosa and bulimia probably represent the most extreme of conflicts between the two eaters within you—your body and your mind. These life-threatening illnesses have afflicted millions in recent times, and a large body of research—mostly in the behavioral sciences —has grown up around them.

Like alcoholism, family violence, and other domestic problems, bulimia and anorexia have come out of hiding. In the past, neither those who had these illnesses nor those who knew someone who did spoke about them. But today you can witness the stories of those who have suffered from bulimia or anorexia almost daily in women's magazines, on TV talk shows, and at community lectures. Note, however, that these are the stories of those who *have* suffered, because one of the symptoms of those caught in the throes of the diseases is *denial.* Denial is the refusal to admit to oneself or others that one is suffering or that one has a specific problem. Because the sufferers themselves characteristically deny their illness, many receive no treatment until their health is seriously threatened.

ANOREXIA
NERVOSA

Anorexia nervosa is an eating disorder characterized by a body weight less than 85 percent of what is considered normal, a distorted body image, an exaggerated fear of being fat, and (in females) the absence of three consecutive menstrual periods.[1] These symptoms are accompanied by self-starving behavior that can lead to severe emaciation and even death.

Although anorectics are starving themselves, they would be the last people to think so. Experts have described how anorectics seem incapable of noticing that they are wasting away. They are likely to spend an unusual amount of time in front of mirrors or on the scale, but they strongly believe that they are fat. This belief can persist long past the point at which others become concerned and even terrified by their skeletal figures and their fragility. And at those times when anorectics can admit that they have lost weight, they usually express a sense of pride and even conceit about this accomplishment, despite the fact that everyone else can see they have gone overboard.

Although anorectics eat very little, most of them claim to feel no hunger. Most also submit themselves to strict exercise regimens, which continue long past the time that their wasting bodies are able to handle them. But anorectics are compelled toward strict physical discipline and always keep active. They are able to do this by drawing on a sense of exaltation and energy they get by not eating. Perfectionism is a driving force in this illness, and most anoretics feel that they must strive for superiority.[2]

Anorectic women stop menstruating at some point in the course of their illness. It has not yet been determined without a doubt why this symptom occurs. While some have suggested that they stop menstruating because of weight loss, it has been found that 30 percent of anorectic patients stop menstruating before any weight loss has even occurred. Certain researchers have suggested that the cessation of menstruation may be due to changes in the hypothalamus, which, as you have read, is involved in the regulation of eating patterns.[3] This could be one clue to a physical basis for the disease.

Anorectics normally engage in bizarre rituals in the preparation, handling, and eating of food. Some are obsessed with eating the same food day after day partly because they have severely reduced the list of foods they consider "ok" to eat. Others have a special way of cutting, weighing, and cooking the food they eat.

About 90 percent of reported anorectics are women. Most, but not all, recorded cases are white and are from middle- or upper-middle-class families. However, there is some evidence that this illness is underdiagnosed in minority groups. About 1 percent of all women between puberty and thirty years of age suffer from anorexia.[4]

Anorexia often first occurs in females near the onset of adolescence. It has been found that many of its victims have mothers who suffered from some eating disorder when they themselves were adolescents. The illness commonly makes its appearance after a dramatic change at home, such as a family death, illness, or separation. Anorexia is closely associated with the atmosphere of the family, and the majority of anorectics unconsciously feel that they play a key role in keeping family dynamics functioning.

Most experts would agree that the anorectic is someone who suffers from low self-esteem and an inability to think of herself as separate from her family. This inability is traced to early childhood, during which she experienced conflicts about her dependence on and attempts to be independent from her mother. A lot of these conflicts might have been set up originally in the context of being fed. It has even been suggested that the anorectic's inability to recognize hunger stems from her having been fed by a mother who was not sensitive to her individual needs for feeding and other nurturing behavior.

According to some theorists, in reality, the families of anorectics are often heavily dependent on *them*. A majority of the mothers of anorectics are portrayed as individuals who have a strong need to attach their daughters to them. These mothers themselves are extremely dependent, but, without realizing it, they express their dependence by fostering dependence in their daughters. The mother's dependence is not a conscious reality in the mind of the anorectic. But in some deep sense she is bothered by a feeling of responsibility for her mother's happiness. At the same time, she feels like the weak one in the relationship, which is played out as if it were still between infant and parent.

In many cases of anorexia, a person's refusal to eat is a way of saying no to a mother or other key family member. Since being fed was the primary bond for mother and child at the period of greatest closeness in their relationship, refusing to eat becomes a way of breaking ties with the mother. Self-starvation is in a sense a bid for independence. But anorectics feel *ambivalent* about the issue of dependence/independence. Thus, not eating serves a triple need. At the same time that it severs connection between the anorectic and those she feels dependent on, it attracts their attention and arouses their concern—thus strengthening the bond in a certain way. Finally, it punishes the anorectic, who feels hopelessly guilty for her desire to break away and be independent.

In a sense, the adolescent anorectic may also be

denying her passage into maturity by refusing to have the body of a woman. Wasting of the body makes hips, buttocks, and breasts melt away. The anorectic achieves a certain unisex identity that is neither male nor female.[5] Doing so may betray certain fears about being sexual and attracting men. Refusing to have a mature body could be a way in which an anorectic avoids competing with her mother. She may even unconsciously fear that the development of her body is a threat to her mother because it could arouse the masculine attentions of her father.

In the deadly dance played out between an anorectic and her family, there are no real villains or victims. Neither the anorectic nor her mother nor other family members wish to do harm to one another. But patterns of dependence, rebellion, and self-blame have caught all players in a grip that can only be severed when real feelings are experienced, expressed, and understood.

THE PHYSICAL RISKS OF ANOREXIA

It is important for anyone suffering from anorexia to get help as soon as possible. Some mild cases respond merely by having weight, eating habits, and diet monitored weekly by a physician. But others may require psychotherapy, medication for depression, or daily attendance in a self-help group.[6] Untreated anorexia risks death. About one in ten victims of anorexia dies from the disease.[7]

The most common cause of death from anorexia is heart failure. This is the result of advanced starvation, when the body begins to live off muscle tissue, including the muscle tissue of the heart.[8] Other effects include yellowing of the skin, which is caused by eating too many vegetables and fruits containing carotene; brittle nails; thinning hair; and dry skin. The loss of body fat in the anorectic often leads to the inability to tolerate cold. As a compensation, the body sometimes grows a fine layer of hair over its surface. Periods stop, and there is a loss of interest in sex.[9]

THE DANGER SIGNALS OF ANOREXIA

In their newsletter, the American Anorexia/Bulimia Association lists the following signs indicating that a person may be developing anorexia:

o loss of a great deal of weight in a relatively short period

o continuing to diet, although bone-thin

o reaching diet goal and then immediately setting another for further weight loss

o dissatisfaction with appearance, even after reaching weight loss goal

o preferring to diet in isolation rather than joining a group

o loss of monthly menstrual periods

o strange eating rituals and/or eating extremely small amounts of food

o becoming a secret eater

o being obsessive about exercising

o long-lasting depressions

o binging and purging

BULIMIA

About half of the victims of anorexia also suffer from bulimia.[10] Bulimia is defined as regular episodes of binging followed by forced vomiting, using laxatives or diuretics, fasting or strict dieting, and/or strenuous exercise in an attempt to burn off calories. The person would also feel a lack of control over eating habits and be overly concerned about the body's shape and weight.[11]

Most of the 50 percent of bulimics who are not anorectic are of near-normal weight.[12] As a result, they are able to hide their disease from others. Few of these bulimics also suffer from cessation of menstruation, although menstrual irregularity is common.[13]

As in anorexia, the majority, but not all, of the victims are white, female, and from middle- or upper-middle-class backgrounds. The number of people afflicted by bulimia is slightly higher than for anorexia. Recent studies have found that 3 to 5 percent of all women between puberty and age thirty have suffered from periods of bulimia.[14]

In bulimics, ambivalence finds a clearer expression than in any of the other eating disorders. As eating disorder specialist Kathy Bowen-Woodward has pointed out, "The bulimic wants to have her cake and eat it too. . . . She wants to eat all that she craves, but she doesn't want to get fat. . . . But once again, the solution isn't so perfect. . . . What began as something she elected to do becomes something she has to do."[15]

Again the issue of control is essential here. The anorectic has the appearance of being overdisciplined—too much in control. But the bulimic rides a roller coaster of changing moods and behavior. She feels disturbingly out of control when she binges. She is often plagued by fits of depression and deep remorse. She is constantly shifting from an almost religious abstention from food to an orgy of eating. This is then reversed by the process of voiding the foods by vomiting or taking laxatives.

A bulimic feels most in control when she fasts or follows a strict diet, but this is also the time when she feels most deprived. Binging fills the hole of deprivation within her and momentarily connects her to her environment. Then this feeling is soon overshadowed by the shame and fear she feels at giving in to her impulses and losing control. Making herself vomit up the food is her way of reestablishing control over her body and rejecting the substance that made her feel needy and dependent.

At least half of bulimics come from a family where alcohol was a problem. And the bulimic herself may have problems with alcohol or drugs. As in anorexia, bulimia often indicates a strong conflict about being nurtured and about feeling dependent. The same parent/daughter conflicts that hold true for anorectics usually hold true for bulimics. The bulimic is merely acting them out in a different way. While the anorectic has chosen one stoic solution to the ambivalence she feels, the bulimic shifts continually between the two poles.

It is possible to die from bulimia. In a few cases, constant vomiting leads to an electrolyte imbalance that causes heart failure. Bulimics may also rupture their esophagus or choke to death while vomiting.[16] Some use more and more desperate measures to induce the vomiting reflex.

Other health problems sometimes result from the practice of bulimia. The vomiting causes sores in the mouth and eventually rots teeth. Gums swell, and the salivary glands enlarge. Vomiting and use of laxatives create digestive disturbances or muscle spasms in the hands and feet. Because bulimics often eat as much as five thousand calories in one binge, their abdominal muscles may be stretched, producing a bloated look.

THE
DANGER SIGNALS
OF BULIMIA

In their newsletter, the American Anorexia/Bulimia Association lists the following signs indicating that a person may be developing bulimia:

o   regular binging (eating large amounts of food over a short period of time)

o   regular purges (by vomiting, diuretics, laxatives, strict dieting, or excessive exercising)

o   retaining or regaining weight despite frequent exercise and dieting

o   not gaining weight but eating enormous amounts of food at one sitting

o   disappearing into the bathroom for long periods of time to induce vomiting

o   abusing drugs or alcohol or stealing regularly

o   long periods of depression

o   irregular menstrual periods

o   dental problems, swollen cheek glands, bloating, or scars on the backs of the hands from forced vomiting

ANOREXIA
AND BULIMIA:
A FEMINIST INTERPRETATION

As you have read, anorexia and bulimia are usually interpreted in the light of a person's family dynamics. Although physical causes, such as abnormality in the hypothalamus, have been suggested, there is still too little data on them to be of much use to sufferers. Recently, however, a new dimension has been added to the psychological causes of bulimia and anorexia. Some theorists of eating disorders have been describing these diseases in the context of society as a whole.

In her book *The Hungry Self: Women, Eating, and Identity*, Kim Chernin looks at anorexia and other eating disorders from a feminist perspective. Of special interest to her is the high percentage of females afflicted by these diseases and the special role of the mother/daughter relationship. Her analysis of the diseases points out some striking differences in expectations about the maturation of boys and girls in our culture. Whereas boys are encouraged to compete and are congratulated if they surpass their fathers in career achievements, income, and standard of living, girls are usually not expected to compete with their mothers. Thus, it is often much easier for boys to deal with feelings of independence or rebellion without the attendant guilt.

Theorists Denise M. Montero and Dodi C. Ardalan concur with Chernin. They also maintain that women are trained to locate the source of control in their lives outside themselves and "to depend upon others to evaluate their course of action."[17] Women, especially those with eating disorders, are more likely to evaluate their looks and general attractiveness according to others' opinions, which makes them feel passive and helpless when it comes to mastering bodily functions.

Judith McNeely, a psychologist at the University of Wisconsin Hospital, goes so far as to insist that eating disorders be looked at as behaviors that are socially learned rather than as medical diseases. She puts eating disorders in the same category as alcoholism and then poses the question of why eating disorders affect ten women for every man, whereas male alcoholics surpass females by a four-to-one ratio.

According to her, both behaviors were learned

and are a product of gender expectations in our society. Women have always been associated with the preparation and serving of food. This is traditionally one of their main realms for expressing creativity and mastery. They have, conversely, been taught that it is less acceptable for them to drink, whereas heavy drinking for men has often been portrayed as part of an acceptable rite of passage into manhood.[18]

Such considerations may not cure the anorectic or bulimic, but they serve to widen the perspective on these disorders. At present, insight is the best tool for dealing with conflicts and pitfalls. Insight and understanding offer the sufferer a feeling of control, which can act as a first step in putting an end to the cycles of temptation and self-blame characteristic of all eating disorders.

Getting Help

FACING AND CONTROLLING AN EATING DISORDER

Eating disorders are a challenge coming from one's true feelings and true self. For the problem eater, they are a voice begging to be heard, an identity striving to be known. But in every case, the identity is masked and the voice is a disguised one. It takes courage and determination to unveil what is really being expressed by an eating disorder. The first step in this process is being able to admit that one has a problem.

RELINQUISHING SELF-BLAME

This first step in getting treatment for an eating disorder is, of course, the most difficult. If eating disorders are caused by low self-esteem, then defining oneself as "having a problem" might seem like a confirmation of this negative image. Avowal of a problem seems negative, however, because people with eating disorders tend to blame themselves for their problems.

You have already seen how the problem eater's

shame and self-blame can stem from negative experiences in childhood that were in reality not the person's fault. Getting help for an eating disorder stops being a shameful avowal of weakness or imperfection the moment a person stops blaming herself for those early unpleasant experiences. Relinquishing self-blame is like taking the cork out of an overcharged bottle. It gives the person the right to identify, express, and understand heretofore suppressed feelings.

The torrent of feelings that come out when a person faces an eating disorder can be very threatening. That is why guidance and support is absolutely necessary. Fortunately, many kinds of treatment and support for eating disorders have become available in recent years. The next sections describe some of them.

HELP
FOR LIGHT
EATING DISORDERS

The kind of therapy that a person with an eating disorder chooses to receive should depend in part on the severity of the disorder. The goals are for the patient to be able to explore the inner causes of her problem at the same time that she receives support and encouragement to battle her low self-esteem. In addition, practical measures to control the behavior and ensure physical health must be instituted. Sometimes these requirements temporarily work against each other. For example, a person with a severe eating disorder who suffers from deep feelings of guilt and low self-confidence might require encouragement more than insight at the beginning. Confronting long-misunderstood feelings would be too traumatic at this time.

On the other hand, those with light eating disorders might lack the motivation to go into deep analysis of their feelings. Compulsive overeaters who do not practice bulimia, people who are obese but do not have serious psychological problems, and anorectics in early stages often benefit from short-term, goal-oriented therapy that places minimal emphasis on the deep-rooted causes of the eating disorder. Instead, it uses a variety of techniques to increase self-esteem, to make the patient more aware of the feelings that go on during problem eating, and to find practical ways to avoid situations that trigger the problem eating behavior.

Short-term therapy for mild eating disorders is usually offered by a social worker, a clinical psychologist, or a behavioral therapist. At the same time, a physician can give diet counseling and monitor weight loss if necessary. People with mild eating disorders who decide to seek professional help for their problem usually encounter one or several of the techniques explained below.

Sound weight-loss management

Physicians, nutritionists, and weight-loss counselors can provide controlled, full-nutrient diets for people suffering from various levels of obesity. These range from balanced diets of 1,400 calories for the mildly overweight to very low calorie liquid diets of from four hundred to eight hundred calories for the significantly obese.

In the case of the very low calorie diet, it is absolutely essential that the dieter be under the close supervision of a physician. These diets, which consist of dissolvable powder derived from egg or milk products, contain essential nutrients with high-quality protein. They are designed to produce the greatest weight loss possible without endangering lean muscle tissue. Dieters take the powder with vitamin and mineral supplements and, in some cases, also eat small portions of lean meat. They also are instructed to drink at least 2 quarts (1.9 liters) of water a day. In addition, their blood must be monitored for its electrolyte balance every other week.

Very low calorie diets cause weight loss in almost all very obese people. An average woman can lose about 3 pounds (1.3 kg) a week; a man, about 4½ pounds (2 kg) a week. Afterward, they are instructed as to how to return slowly to eating normal foods. In every case, medical supervision is required for weight loss, for going back to normal foods, and for maintaining the weight later.

Group Support

This technique is based on the assumption that people with similar problems can give each other support and encouragement. It generally consists of a group of people, ranging from five to twenty individuals, who share a tendency toward problem eating. The group usually meets once a week. It is monitored by a psychotherapist who encourages the members to freely express their conflicts about eating, to bond together to increase mutual self-esteem, and to confront one another about the need to face the true nature of their disorder.

Behavioral Therapy

This technique stresses the need to control the symptoms of eating disorders. It is based on the understanding that as long as a patient focuses all energy and thinking on carrying out the actions of problem eating, she will not become motivated toward the process of self-examination and change.[1]

In this type of therapy, insight is not the major goal. Instead, the individual attempts to retrain habits by a variety of means. These range from steps to practice for the cooking, serving, and eating of a meal to steps for avoiding situations in which the eating problem normally occurs.

A common behavioral technique in the treatment of compulsive overeating or mild bulimia is to have the individual write down everything she eats, where and when she eats it, and her accompanying feelings. The therapist then accumulates information as to the exact situation in which the behavior occurs and discusses practical ways of avoiding this pattern in the future.

There are also semitherapeutic methods of behavior therapy offered by such organizations as Weight-Watchers. These organizations offer the dieter the chance to set a weight-loss goal, get group encouragement, plan a sensible diet, and learn little tricks to avoid overeating, such as putting a warning sign on the refrigerator, calling a partner for support whenever the desire to binge is felt, or learning to eat more slowly and take smaller bites.

Certain clinics offer the option of aversion therapy. In aversion therapy, a person is shown plates or pictures of a specific problem food or bad eating habits and given a mild electric shock at the same time in an attempt to recondition the bad habits.

Stress Reduction

Problem eating often increases when a person comes under stress. People regularly turn to food as a possible remedy for stressful feelings. But in the case of the problem eater, this remedy only serves to increase the stress level.[2]

Short-term psychotherapists try to relieve stress by developing coping behaviors. They ask people to examine how they react in certain situations and to choose a behavior that leads to less stress. They also offer relaxation techniques such as breathing and stretching exercises, self-hypnosis, and biofeedback.

Exercise

Professionals seeking to provide a total program for the correction of mild eating disorders usually include exercise as a component. Moderate, regular exercise holds several benefits for problem eaters. It keeps the body toned and increases energy. It is a proven stress reducer and gives the exerciser a general sense of well-being. The benefits of exercise do much to combat a problem eater's sense of body inferiority. However, in some eating disorders, especially anorexia and bulimia, exercise itself can become a problem. If too much exercise or exercise as a form of self-punishment is already an element of an individual's eating disorder, a therapist may want to avoid emphasis on this kind of behavior.

Cognitive Restructuring

Cognitive restructuring means working to give new meaning to a person's system of thought. The process consists of training the individual to identify negative beliefs and to substitute positive and realistic statements for them. Sheila A. Ramsey, a therapist who works with eating disorders, calls such negative beliefs "negative self-talk" and has defined their components as follows:[3]

1. Catastrophizing—seeing the situation in its worst perspective.

2. Overgeneralizing—drawing conclusions based on limited information.

3. Black-and-white thinking—you are either perfect or a failure.

4. "Should" statements—setting up "musts" for oneself or others frequently leads to guilt or anger.

5. Self-referencing—believing your actions (mistakes) are noticed by others.

6. Filtering—focusing on the negative aspects of a situation or yourself.

With cognitive restructuring, the individual practices becoming aware of "negative self-talk" and gets help from the therapist on how to revise unproductive attitudes.

HELP
FOR SERIOUS
EATING DISORDERS

In the case of anorectics or bulimics, more intensive styles of therapy are usually necessary. In some cases, medical supervision for the physical effects of the disease is also given. For example, a bulimic might need to have her blood electrolytes tested regularly. And an anorectic will require someone to keep an eye on her weight changes and food intake.

People with serious eating disorders sometimes benefit from the full battery of treatments. They may need to see a psychotherapist who slowly and encouragingly helps them delve deeply into the nature of their problem while they try to retrain behavior and learn new habits. At the same time, membership in a support group of others with the same problem may also be of benefit. Antidepressant drugs may be needed and can be prescribed by a physician. Intensive therapy is usually begun by a clinical psychologist, a psychiatric social worker, or a psychiatrist. Any one of these professionals may also have training in psychoanalysis.

In many cases, the family is called in to help. Family therapy has been shown to be very effective in the treatment of anorexia at the Ackerman Institute for Family Therapy in New York City and at other family clinics.

In the case of this kind of therapy, the behavior of the patient is not seen as individual but as part of a larger system. The goal of the therapy is to try to determine what pattern of family relationships the behavior of the anorectic is working to uphold. Doing so involves asking other family members to attend therapy sessions with the anorectic and to be forthcoming. The difficulty is in getting family members to realize and admit their role in the eating disorder. In many cases, denial on the part of family members is even stronger than in the patient showing the symptoms.

EMERGENCY MEASURES

For severely anorectic or bulimic individuals, hospitalization may be the only answer. If a person is seriously weakened by starvation, she will not be able to sustain any kind of probing psychotherapy. Instead, her physical needs must be met immediately. In such cases, the patient may first be fed intravenously. If her life is seriously threatened, she may be force-fed by a method of tube-feeding called *hyperalimentation.* This is a surgical procedure in which a tube is inserted into a vein above the anorectic's heart. Liquid nourishment is then pumped through the tube directly into the bloodstream.

In an inpatient psychiatric ward, the person with a severe eating disorder will probably be assigned a psychiatrist, who will prescribe and oversee medication. A social worker will take a family history and will supervise the daily group therapy sessions in which the patient is expected to participate. Other therapeutic personnel, such as psychologists, nurses, and program coordinators will be called in as needed.

In the inpatient ward, the anorectic becomes subject to certain rules of behavior. The treatment team begins to challenge her image of herself as fat and encourages her to eat. If she is bulimic, self-purging will be firmly discouraged. And if necessary, pressure to stop dangerous behavior will be maximized. For example, eating properly may be tied to the privilege of exercising, of watching television, or of leaving on weekend passes. The patient may be asked to sign a behavioral contract in which she agrees to abide by certain rules or to suffer the consequences. In this way the patient becomes part of a community of people with similar problems who live by the same rules, which is a challenge to her isolation and alienation.[4] Once she is out of danger, she can begin participating in more probing, self-directed kinds of therapy.

What follows below is an actual behavioral contract between one especially difficult bulimic inpatient and her treatment team. Because her behavior presented serious dangers to herself and was disruptive to others, she was asked to abide by the contract in return for receiving treatment at the hospital. You may not agree with these kinds of emergency measures. The therapeutic team acknowledged the fact that the contract put limits on the patient's freedom and self-expression. But they felt it was justified because it endorsed the kind of behavior that would be expected of an individual in the outside world.

BEHAVIORAL CONTRACT[5]

Name: Nancy
Date: 10/10/92
Week of hospitalization: 4th

I. Eating

A. Goal Behaviors
1. Patient will eat all food on her tray at all meals.
2. Patient will not eat any food other than in #1.
3. Patient will meet twice weekly with the dietician to plan meals.
4. Patient will not vomit or engage in unauthorized physical exercise.

B. Consequences
1. If the patient accomplishes 1–4 through 10/17/92, bathroom will be left unlocked after meals and one-to-one nursing observation during meals will be discontinued.

2. Failure to accomplish 1–4 will result in bathroom remaining locked for two hours after meals and continued one-to-one nursing observation during meals.
3. If patient is found exercising in her room, further restrictions (one-to-one in room; lock out of room except between 11 P.M. and 7 A.M.; loss of recreation room privilege) may be imposed at the discretion of the program coordinator.

II. Self-injury

A. Goal Behaviors
   1. Patient will not cause injury to herself by cutting, scratching, bruising herself, etc.
   2. Patient will express feelings and self-destructive impulses verbally to a member of the treatment team or to co-patients during group therapy.
   3. Patient may use punching dummy with supervision at discretion of nursing staff.

B. Consequences
   1. If patient accomplishes 1–3 through 10/17/92, she will be allowed to go on bowling and movie trips.
   2. Self-injury will result in confinement to the unit for a minimum of seven days.
   3. Additional restrictions and/or loss of privileges may be imposed at the discretion of the program coordinator.

III. Aggressive Behavior

A. Goal Behaviors
   1. Patient will express anger verbally in assertive, nonblameful and nonthreatening ways.
   2. Patient will not physically or verbally abuse or threaten any other person.
      a. Any member of the hospital staff is authorized to determine whether a particular behavior is abusive or threatening.
   3. Patient will not physically act out anger toward inanimate objects (e.g., throwing, kicking, punching, slamming doors, etc.).

4. Patient may use punching dummy with supervision at the discretion of the nursing staff.

B. Consequences same as II.

HOW YOU CAN HELP A PERSON WITH AN EATING DISORDER

Now that you know some of the causes, symptoms, and treatments for eating disorders, you will probably become more aware of them in others. There is a good chance that you now know someone suffering from compulsive overeating, anorexia, or bulimia. What behavior on your part will be most helpful to that person? Answering this question completely depends upon your personality, the personality of the person suffering from the disorder, and your relationship to that person. However, the following general guidelines may be of some help:

1. *Don't be critical.* As you now know, people with eating disorders suffer from low self-esteem. Jokes, exaggerated concern, or harsh criticism about the body can be especially damaging to them. There are ways to express honest concern without making the person feel judged or diminished. But keep in mind that denial is often an important component of an eating disorder. Arguing with someone who refuses to acknowledge an eating disorder will not do that person any good.

2. *Don't enable.* People who practice unhealthy eating often covertly depend on people without eating disorders. Though you yourself do not have an eating disorder, you may be a *co-dependent* of someone who suffers from one. A co-dependent is someone who helps a person to carry out unhealthy or addictive behavior.

Without your knowing it, a friend or family member with an eating disorder may need you to maintain the behavior. This need may be expressed in very subtle ways. For example, a girlfriend may go on an eating binge every time you have an argument with her. A best friend may binge as long as you are there to find his pigging out hilarious. A sister may starve herself because you are able to get all of your parents' attention for yourself.

Co-dependency is complicated. You may never understand your role in another person's eating disorder until that person has worked it out in a therapeutic setting, with or without you. However, it is often helpful to remain aware of the possibility that you play a role in a friend's or family member's problems with food.

3. *Be there.* In those cases where a person with an eating disorder is able to ask for help, it is an advantage to be prepared. Educating yourself about the signs of eating disorders and where one can go for help may come in handy. However, don't push this information on a person suffering from an eating disorder. In such a case, your insistence may do more harm then good.

4. *Don't blame yourself.* Whether you are a co-dependent or not, the final responsibility for curing an eating disorder rests with the person who has it. One rule of thumb to follow is that no one is to blame. This prevents not only blaming yourself but projecting that feeling of blame onto others.

5. *Show compassion.* An eating disorder is an illness. Supportiveness, patience, and acceptance of the person suffering from it may be the best medicine. If the person suffering from an eating disorder feels that you care and that you understand, it will boost self-esteem and bring the person closer to self-

acceptance. Self-acceptance is the first major step toward curing an eating disorder.

DEALING WITH RELAPSES

Once treatment has been successful, does that mean the eating disorder has become a problem of the past? Not in most cases. A new approach to treating eating disorders now focuses on *relapses,* or slips. According to Howard J. Shaffer, a psychologist at the Center for Addiction Studies at Harvard Medical School, "For any habit you want to change, the key to success is not just stopping, but keeping from relapsing." Dr. Shaffer believes that a relapse is essentially a positive experience because "you can learn from a slip how to keep it from happening again."

Shaffer's emphasis on the positive side of relapsing is in direct contrast to past attitudes about lapsing, which made individuals feel that if they made one mistake, they were back to square one. Lately, methods of dealing with relapses after treatment have received as much attention as the treatment process itself. G. Allan Marlatt, a psychologist at the University of Washington who specializes in breaking habits, sees a slip from supposedly cured behavior as "an error in learning, not a failure in willpower. The belief that a slip means you have no willpower or are addicted is a self-fulfilling prophecy. . . . But people who recover from habits they want to change treat slips very differently . . . recovering from a slip gives them a stronger confidence in their ability to resist temptation."

Marlatt identifies those people who go back to bad behavior as people who blame themselves for a lapse rather than blaming the situation. They are filled with guilt and therefore are unable to return to a pattern of healthy behavior. He favors advising people who slip that they are more than likely to feel guilt and self-blame. They should allow this to pass until they can review the situation and discover their mood, the people they were with, and where they were when the slip occurred. Knowing these elements will help them to identify potential problem situations in the future. Then the sequence of events can be interrupted before the slip reoccurs.[6]

Twelve-step programs, such as Overeaters Anonymous, have proved of enormous benefit, both for those struggling to overcome eating disorders and for those who are prey to relapses. Most of these groups are patterned on Alcoholics Anonymous, a fellowship of self-help that was established in the 1930s. The members of Alcoholics Anonymous recognize no central authority or permanent group leader. They also promise complete anonymity to their members. This means that information about the lives of members never leaves the circle of the group.

Other twelve-step programs, with names like Narcotics Anonymous and Gamblers Anonymous, have sought to apply the principles of Alcoholics Anonymous to all types of addiction. The principle behind these groups is outlined in a credo of twelve steps to which all members subscribe. One of the main features is the necessity of finally admitting that one feels powerless over the addiction.

Once recognition of control as being outside is accomplished, the individual is supposed to invest faith in a higher power. For some members, this higher power is God, but for others it is merely an abstract entity that widens their perspective. Members work to raise each other's self-esteem and to serve as examples of what this can do for a person who wishes to leave behind addictive behavior.

As you have read about the various therapies and helping groups for eating disorders, you may have noticed that most share a common idea. All of them believe that mastery of an eating disorder is largely based on self-knowledge and self-esteem.

Today it is no longer believed that individuals with eating disorders are weak people who are suffering from a defect in character. Neither do most professionals subscribe to the old notion that recovering from an eating disorder is the result of superior willpower. Because eating disorders are believed to stem from ingrained, largely unconscious fears about nurturing and love, the goal of most therapies is to put the problem eater in touch with his or her emotions, to uncover and heal unresolved conflicts. In light of this, anyone with an eating disorder is now asked to embark on a voyage of self-discovery where the only real risk is in coming face to face with oneself.

FINDING TREATMENT
FOR EATING DISORDERS:
REFERRAL ORGANIZATIONS

American Anorexia/Bulimia
Association
418 East 76th Street
New York, New York 10021
Tel. (212) 734-1114

National Anorectic Aid
Society
5796 Karl Road
Columbus, Ohio 43229
Tel. (614) 895-2009

National Association of
Anorexia Nervosa
and Associated Disorders
Box 7
Highland Park, Illinois
60035
Tel. (312) 831-3438

Anorexia Nervosa and
Related Eating Disorders, Inc.
Box 5102
Eugene, Oregon 97405
Tel. (503) 344-1144

Bulimia/Anorexia Self-Help
Deaconess Hospital
6150 Oakland Avenue
St. Louis, Missouri 63139
Tel. (314) 991-BASH
or (800) BAS-HSTL

Anorexics, Bulimics
Anonymous National Service
Office
P.O. Box 47573
Phoenix, Arizona 85968
Tel. (602) 861-3295

GLOSSARY

Ambivalence. A simultaneous attraction to and repulsion from something.

Anorexia nervosa (self-starvation). An eating-disorder disease that involves the practice of eating little or no food for extended periods of time.

Binge eating (compulsive overeating). The practice of eating too much food or of not being able to stop eating.

Binging and purging (see **Bulimia**).

Brown adipose tissue ("brown fat"). A kind of fat known to increase when the body is constantly exposed to cold.

Bulimia (binging and purging). The practice of eating large amounts of food and then eliminating them by vomiting or using laxatives or enemas.

Bulimia nervosa. An eating disorder that involves the regular practice of bulimia.

Compulsive. Irresistibly drawn to something or to a pattern of behavior.

Compulsive overeating (see **Binge eating**).

Densitometry. Dividing the weight of the body by the volume of water it displaces to determine the weight per unit of volume; one way of measuring body fat.

Depression. An emotional state characterized by a lack of energy, a lingering sadness, and a loss of ambition.

Eating disorder. Any habit involving the intake of food that is detrimental to the body over the long haul.

Ectomorph. A slender and light-boned person.

Endocrinologist. A physician who specializes in the diagnosis and treatment of glandular diseases.

Endomorph. A heavy and rounded person.

Hyperalimentation. A method of feeding in which a tube is inserted into a vein above the heart to pump nourishment into the bloodstream.

Hypothalamus. A part of the brain involved in the regulation of eating patterns.

Lipoprotein lipase. An enzyme produced by body tissues that is important in the metabolism of certain fats and fat proteins.

Mesomorph. A stocky and muscular person.

Obese. Significantly overweight (more than thirty pounds [13.5 kg]).

Obsessive. A tendency to become preoccupied with a disturbing or all-absorbing idea.

Purging. Eliminating food by vomiting or using laxatives or enemas.

Relapse. A slip back into an old habit.

Self-starvation (see **Anorexia nervosa**).

Set point. A point at which body metabolism is switched on or off to maintain a certain body weight.

Yo-yo dieting. Repeated, failed attempts at dieting.

SOURCE NOTES

CHAPTER 1
1. Kathy Bowen-Woodward, Ph.D., *Coping with a Negative Body-Image* (New York: Rosen Publishing Group, 1989), p. 31.
2. Kathleen Zraly and David Swift, M.D., *Anorexia, Bulimia, and Compulsive Overeating: A Practical Guide for Counselors and Families* (New York: Continuum, 1990), p. 34.
3. Ibid., p. 77.
4. Ibid., p. 61.

CHAPTER 2
1. Kathy Bowen-Woodward, Ph.D., *Coping with a Negative Body-Image* (New York: Rosen Publishing Group, 1989), p. 12.
2. Dale M. Atrens, Ph.D., *Don't Diet* (New York: William Morrow, 1988), p. 22.
3. Ibid., p. 28.
4. Ibid., p. 29.
5. *Sportsmedicine*, April 1990.

CHAPTER 3
1. Kathleen Zraly and David Swift, M.D., *Anorexia, Bulimia, and Compulsive Overeating: A Practical Guide for Counselors and Families* (New York: Continuum, 1990), p. 26.
2. Ibid., pp. 66–67.
3. Jane E. Brody, "Bulimia and Anorexia: Insidious Eating Disorders That Are Best Treated When Detected Early," *New York Times*, February 22, 1990.
4. Ibid.
5. Denise M. Montero and Dodi C. Ardalan, "Compulsive Eating," in *Weight Control: A Guide for Counselors and Therapists*, ed. Aaron M. Altschul (New York: Praeger, 1987).
6. Ibid.
7. Adapted from Jonathan Kirland Wise, M.D., and Susan

Kierr Wise, *The Overeaters* (New York: Human Sciences Press, 1979), chap. 4.
8. Ibid., p. 62.
9. Ibid.
10. Doreen L. Virtue, *The Yo-Yo Syndrome Diet* (New York: Harper & Row, 1989), pp. 24–25.
11. Ibid., p. 6.
12. Ibid., p. 26.
13. Zraly and Swift, p. 73.
14. Wise and Wise, *The Overeaters*, pp. 114–15.

CHAPTER 4
1. *New York Times*, February 25, 1988, p. A1.
2. Denise Grady, "Is Losing Weight a Losing Battle?"*Time*, March 7, 1988.
3. Adapted from Dale M. Atrens, Ph.D., *Don't Diet* (New York: William Morrow, 1988), chap. 4.
4. Ibid., pp. 101–7.
5. Robert H. Eckel, "Lipoprotein Lipase: A Multifunctional Enzyme Relevant to Common Metabolic Diseases," *New England Journal of Medicine*, April 20, 1989.
6. Williamson et al., "Smoking Cessation and Severity of Weight Gain in a National Cohort," *The New England Journal of Medicine*, 234 (March 14, 1991), p. 739.

CHAPTER 5
1. Dale M. Atrens, Ph.D., *Don't Diet* (New York: William Morrow and Company, 1988), p. 115.
2. Ibid., p. 109.
3. Adapted from Atrens, *Don't Diet*, pp. 112–18.
4. Adapted from Kelly Brownell, "Yo-Yo Dieting," *Psychology Today*, January 1988, pp. 20–23.
5. Questions quoted from Doreen L. Virtue, *The Yo-Yo Syndrome Diet* (New York: Harper & Row, 1989), p. 12.

CHAPTER 6
1. Kathy Bowen-Woodward, Ph.D., *Coping with a Negative Body-Image* (New York: Rosen Publishing Group, 1989), p. 31.
2. Martin A. Ceasar, "Eating Disorders: Anorexia Nervosa and Bulimia," in *Weight Control: A Guide for Counselors and Therapists*, ed. Aaron M. Altschul (New York: Praeger, 1987).

3. Ibid.
4. Jane E. Brody, "Bulimia and Anorexia: Insidious Eating Disorders That Are Best Treated When Detected Early," *New York Times*, February 22, 1990.
5. Ceasar, "Eating Disorders."
6. Brody, "Bulimia and Anorexia."
7. Bowen-Woodward, *Coping*, p. 33.
8. Ibid.
9. Brody, "Bulimia and Anorexia."
10. Ibid.
11. Kathleen Zraly and David Swift, M.D., *Anorexia, Bulimia, and Compulsive Overeating: A Practical Guide for Counselors and Families* (New York: Continuum, 1990), pp. 30–31.
12. Ceasar, "Eating Disorders."
13. Ibid.
14. Brody, "Bulimia and Anorexia."
15. Bowen-Woodward, *Coping*, p. 36.
16. Ibid., p. 37.
17. Denise M. Montero and Dodi C. Ardalan, *Weight Control: A Guide for Counselors and Therapists*, ed. Aaron M. Altschul. (New York: Praeger, 1987).
18. *USA Today*, May 1989, p. 8.

CHAPTER 7
1. Kathleen Zraly and David Swift, M.D., *Anorexia, Bulimia, and Compulsive Overeating: A Practical Guide for Counselors and Families* (New York: Continuum, 1990), p. 87.
2. Sheila A. Ramsey, "Food as a Stressor and as a Stress Reliever: Effectively Managing Stress," *Weight Control: A Guide for Counselors and Therapists*, ed. Aaron M. Altschul (New York: Praeger, 1987).
3. Ibid.
4. Zraly and Swift, *Anorexia*, chap. 5.
5. Ibid., pp. 153–55.
6. Daniel Goleman, "Breaking Bad Habits: New Therapy Focuses on the Relapse," *New York Times*, December 27, 1988.

BIBLIOGRAPHY

BOOKS

Altschul, Aaron M., ed. *Weight Control: A Guide for Counselors and Therapists.* New York: Praeger, 1987.

Atrens, Dale M., Ph.D. *Don't Diet.* New York: William Morrow, 1988.

Bowen-Woodward, Kathy, Ph.D. *Coping with a Negative Body-Image.* New York: Rosen Publishing Group, 1989.

Chernin, Kim. *The Hungry Self: Women, Eating, and Identity.* New York: Random House, 1985.

Claypool, Jane, and Nelsen, Cheryl Diane. *Food Trips and Traps: Coping with Eating Disorders.* New York: Franklin Watts, 1983.

Lee, Sally. *New Theories on Diet and Nutrition.* New York: Franklin Watts: 1990.

Levenkron, S. *The Best Little Girl in the World.* New York: Warner Books, 1979.

Orbach, Susie. *Fat Is a Feminist Issue.* New York: Berkeley, 1978.

Siegel, M., Brisman, J., and Weinshel, M. *Surviving an Eating Disorder: Strategies for Family and Friends.* New York: Harper & Row, 1988.

Virtue, Doreen L. *The Yo-Yo Syndrome Diet.* New York: Harper & Row, 1989.

Wise, Jonathan Kirland, M.D., and Wise, Susan Kierr. *The Overeaters.* New York: Human Sciences Press, 1979.

Zraly, Kathleen, and Swift, David, M.D. *Anorexia, Bulimia, and Compulsive Overeating: A Practical Guide for Counselors and Families.* New York: Continuum, 1990.

ARTICLES

Brody, Jane E. "Bulimia and Anorexia: Insidious Eating Disorders That Are Best Treated When Detected Early." *New York Times*, February 22, 1990.

Brownell, Kelly. "Yo-Yo Dieting." *Psychology Today*, January 1988.

Eckel, Robert H. "Lipoprotein Lipase: A Multifunctional Enzyme Relevant to Common Metabolic Diseases." *The New England Journal of Medicine*, April 20, 1989.

Goldsmith, Marsha F. "Heart Disease Researchers Tailor New Theories—Now Maybe It's Genes That Make People Fat." *The Journal of the American Medical Association*, January 5, 1990.

Goleman, Daniel. "Breaking Bad Habits: New Therapy Focuses on the Relapse." *New York Times*, December 27, 1988.

Grady, Denise. "Is Losing Weight a Losing Battle?" *Time*, March 7, 1988.

Grunberg, Neil E. "Smoking Cessation and Weight Gain." *The New England Journal of Medicine*, March 14, 1991.

"Helping Alcoholics and Bulimics." *USA Today*, May 1989.

"How to Prevent Eating Binges." *USA Today*, December 1989.

King, Peter. "Battle of the Bulge." *Sports Illustrated*, September 2, 1991.

Kolata, Gina. "New Obesity Studies Indicate Metabolism Is Often to Blame." *New York Times*, February 25, 1988.

———. "Vindication for a Leading Proponent of Theory 'People Are Born to Be Fat.' " *New York Times*, February 25, 1988.

O'Donnell, Michael. "A Food Malady That Likes Upwardly Mobile Women." *International Management*, October 1986.

Pike, Kathleen, and Rodin, Judith. "Girls' Anorexia, Bulimia Linked to Mothers' Criticism." *The Washington Post*, April 30, 1991.

Rusting, Ricki. "Starvaholics? Anorexics May Be Addicted to a Starvation 'High.' " *Scientific American*, November 1988.

Sims, Ethan A. H. "Destiny Rides Again as Twins Overeat." *The New England Journal of Medicine,* May 24, 1990.

Stunkard, Albert J.; Harris, J. R.; Pedersen, Nancy L; and McClearn, G. E. "The Body-mass of Twins Who Have Been Reared Apart." *The New England Journal of Medicine,* May 24, 1990.

Thornton, James S. "Feast or Famine: Eating Disorders in Athletes." *Sportsmedicine,* April 1990.

Wadden, A.; Van Italie, Theodore B.; and Blackbrun, George L. "Responsible and Irresponsible Use of Very-Low-Calorie Diets in the Treatment of Obesity. *The Journal of the American Medical Association,* January 5, 1990.

"What Causes Bulimia?" *USA Today,* February 1988.

Williamson et al. "Smoking Cessation and Severity of Weight Gain in a National Cohort." *The New England Journal of Medicine,* 234 (March 14, 1991), p. 739.

INDEX